New Mexico Dreamscapes III

Bobby J. Jones

ISBN:1717143237
ISBN-13:9781717143235

DEDICATION

I dedicate New Mexico Dreamscapes III and its images to the loving memory of my dad Herman Anthony "Toney" Jones.

ACKNOWLEDGMENTS

I WOULD LIKE TO ACKNOWLEDGE THE MEMORY OF MY DAD THE LATE RETIRED USAF LT. COLONEL HERMAN ANTHONY "TONEY' JONES IN THIS COLORING BOOK.

MY DAD WAS BORN ON SEPTEMBER 7, 1932 IN PAMPA, GRAY COUNTY, TEXAS TO JOHN HERMAN JONES AND BONNIE THELMA TURCOTTE JONES. MY DAD WAS THE ONLY SON IN HIS FAMILY. MY DAD HAD AN OLDER SISTER MARGARET J. KENNEDY OF MIDLAND, TEXAS THAT WAS 4 YEARS OLDER THAN HIM.

MY DAD GREW UP IN PAMPA, TEXAS DURING THE HEART OF THE GREAT DEPRESSION. HIS FAMILY SURVIVED THAT ERA IN AMERICAN HISTORY DESPITE MY GRANDFATHER JONES LOSING EVERYTHING. MY DAD'S FATHER WAS A SCHOOL TEACHER AND A FARMER.

MY DAD LOVED PLAYING SPORTS ESPECIALLY BASKETBALL. HE PLAYED BASKETBALL FOR PAMPA HIGH SCHOOL. HE WAS ON THE BASKETBALL TEAM THAT WON THE DISTRICT CHAMPIONSHIP AND LATER PLAYED IN THE STATE PLAYOFFS IN 1950. MY DAD GRADUATED FROM PAMPA HIGH SCHOOL IN 1951.

HE ATTENDED TEXAS TECHNOLOGICAL COLLEGE. HE GRADUATED FROM TEXAS TECH IN 1956 WITH A BA IN BUSINESS ADMINISTRATION. WHILE ATTENDING THIS TEXAS UNIVERSITY IN THE 1950S, HE BECAME A MEMBER OF THE ARNOLD AIR SOCIETY AND ALPHA TAU OMEGA. WHEN MY DAD GRADUATED FROM TEXAS TECH, HE ENLISTED IN THE UNITED STATES AIR FORCE.

MY PARENTS MET AT TEXAS TECH IN THE SPRING OF 1954. MY MOM RODE WITH MY DAD IN MY DAD'S 1941 BLUE FORD CONVERTIBLE TO VISIT ONE OF HER SORIETY SISTERS, WHO LIVED IN PAMPA, TEXAS. AFTER THAT TRIP TO PAMPA, MY PARENTS STARTED DATING. ON OCTOBER 16, 1954, MY PARENTS WERE MARRIED IN LUBBOCK, TEXAS AT THE BROADWAY CHURCH OF CHRIST CHAPEL.

ACCORDING TO MY GRANDMOTHER JONES, MY DAD ALWAYS WANTED TO FLY AIRPLANES SINCE HIS CHILDHOOD. HE WOULD SPEND HOURS BUILDING AIRPLANE MODELS AND HANGING THEM IN HIS CHILDHOOD BEDROOM.

MY DAD TRAINED AS AN USAF PILOT AT ELLINGTON FIELD IN HOUSTON, TEXAS IN 1956. HIS FIRST COMISSION WAS AT MCCHORD AIR FORCE BASE IN 1957. IN 1959, DAD RECEIVED HIS NEXT ASSIGNMENT AT HICKAM AIR FORCE BASE IN HAWAII. THEN IN 1963, MY DAD WAS ASSIGNED TO REESE AIR FORCE BASE IN LUBBOCK, TEXAS.

DURING THIS TIME, MY DAD ATTENDED TEXAS TECHNOLOGICAL COLLEGE. HE BECAME THE ASSISTANT HEAD OFFICER TO ALL THE USAF CADETS AT TEXAS TECH WHILE TEACHING AFROTC AND WORKING TOWARDS HIS MBA IN BUSINESS ADMINISTRATION. MY DAD FINISHED HIS GRADUATE DEGREE IN 1967.

THEN HE RECEIVED HIS ORDERS TO GO TO VIETNAM IN APRIL, 1967. MY DAD WAS A NAVIGATOR AND FLEW TRANSPORT CARGO PLANES TO AND FROM THE DMZ. HE WAS INVOLVED IN THE TET OFFENSIVE IN 1968. MY DAD RETURNED HOME FROM VIETNAM IN AUGUST, 1968.

AFTER RETURNING FROM VIETNAM, MY DAD WAS OFFERED A JOB POSITION AS AN INDUSTRIAL ENGINEER AT GENERAL DYNAMICS IN THE ESTIMATING DEPARTMENT AT THE FORT WORTH, TEXAS PLANT. HE WORKED AT GENERAL DYNAMICS FOR 25 YEARS AND RETIRED IN 1993. MY DAD RETIRED FROM THE UNITED STATES AIR FORCE IN 1984 AS A LIEUTENANT COLONEL.

MY DAD LOVED PLAYING GOLF. WHEN I WAS BORN, MY DAD NAMED ME AFTER THREE FAMOUS PEOPLE, BOBBY JONES (THE GOLFER), JACK KENNEDY, AND BOBBY KENNEDY. MY FULLNAME IS BOBBY JACK JONES.

MY DAD PASSED AWAY ON OCTOBER 2, 1998 FROM A STAGE FOUR CANCEROUS BRAIN TUMOR. HE WENT INTO A SEIZURE AND PASSED AWAY IN MATTER OF SECONDS. HE WAS 66 YEARS OLD.

MY DAD TAUGHT ME MANY THINGS IN LIFE FROM HITTING A BASEBALL TO LEARNINNG HOW TO TIE A NECKTIE. THE ONE THING MY DAD TAUGHT ME FOCUSED UPON THE DISCIPLINE TO CREATE ART. I ALSO DEVELOPED A LOVE FOR MATH AND NUMBERS FROM HIM. WHEN I SEE MATH AND ART, MY DAD'S SPIRIT IS RIGHT THERE WITH ME. HE TELLS ME TO STAY FOCUSED AND PAY ATTENTION. I LOVE YOU AND MISS YOU, DAD!

Contents.

Bobby J. Jones

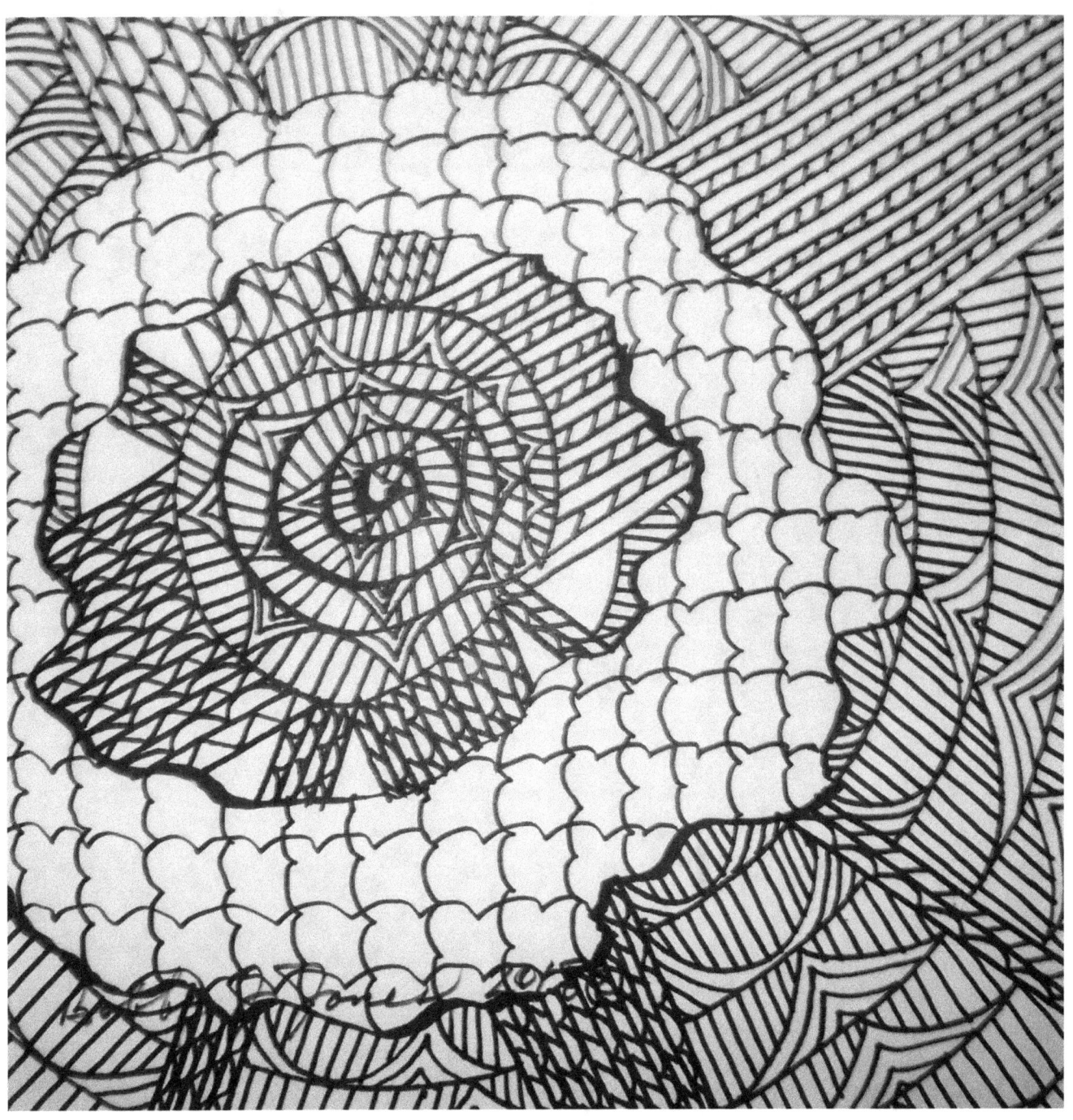

Bobby J. Jones

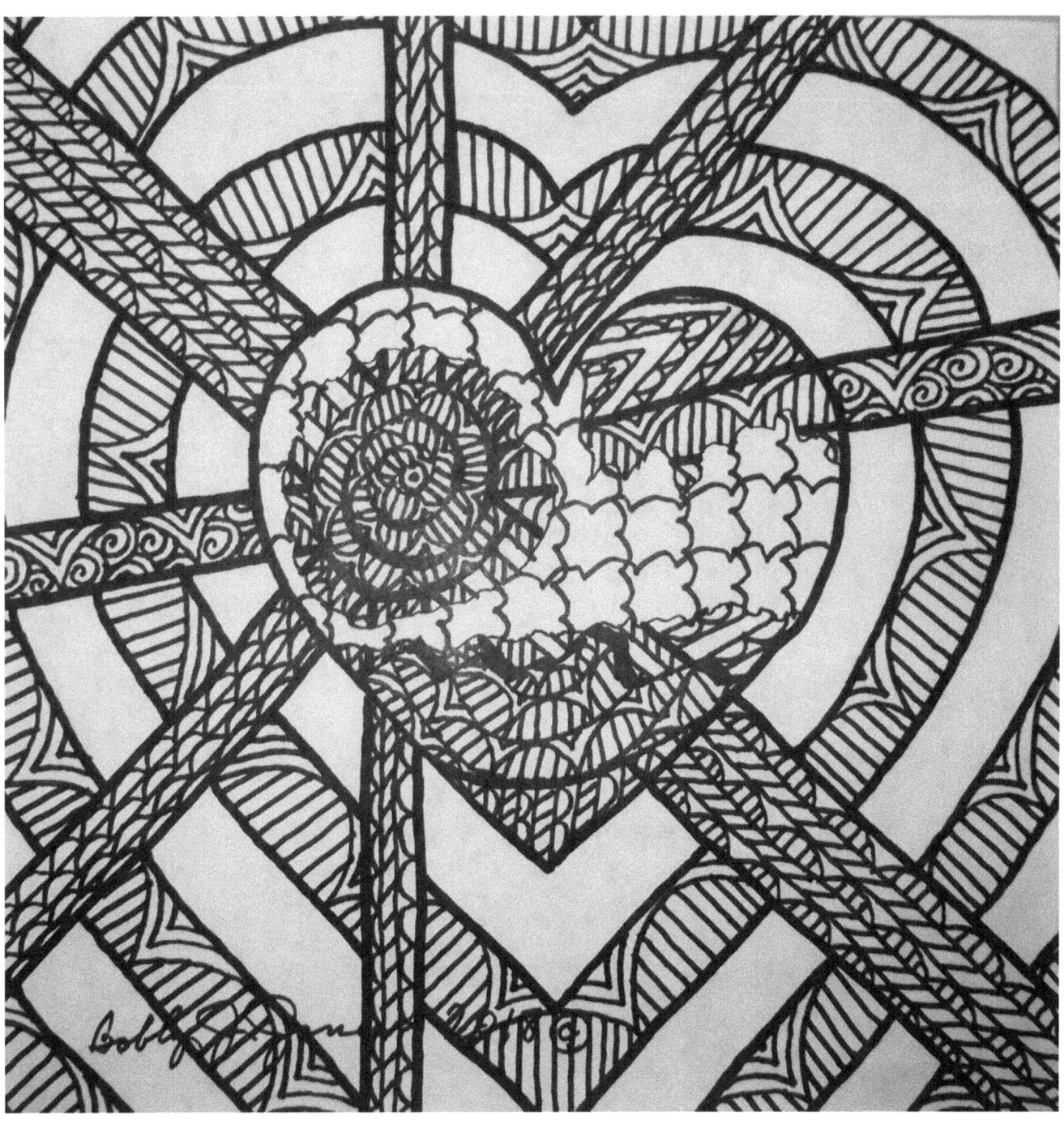

Bobby J. Jones

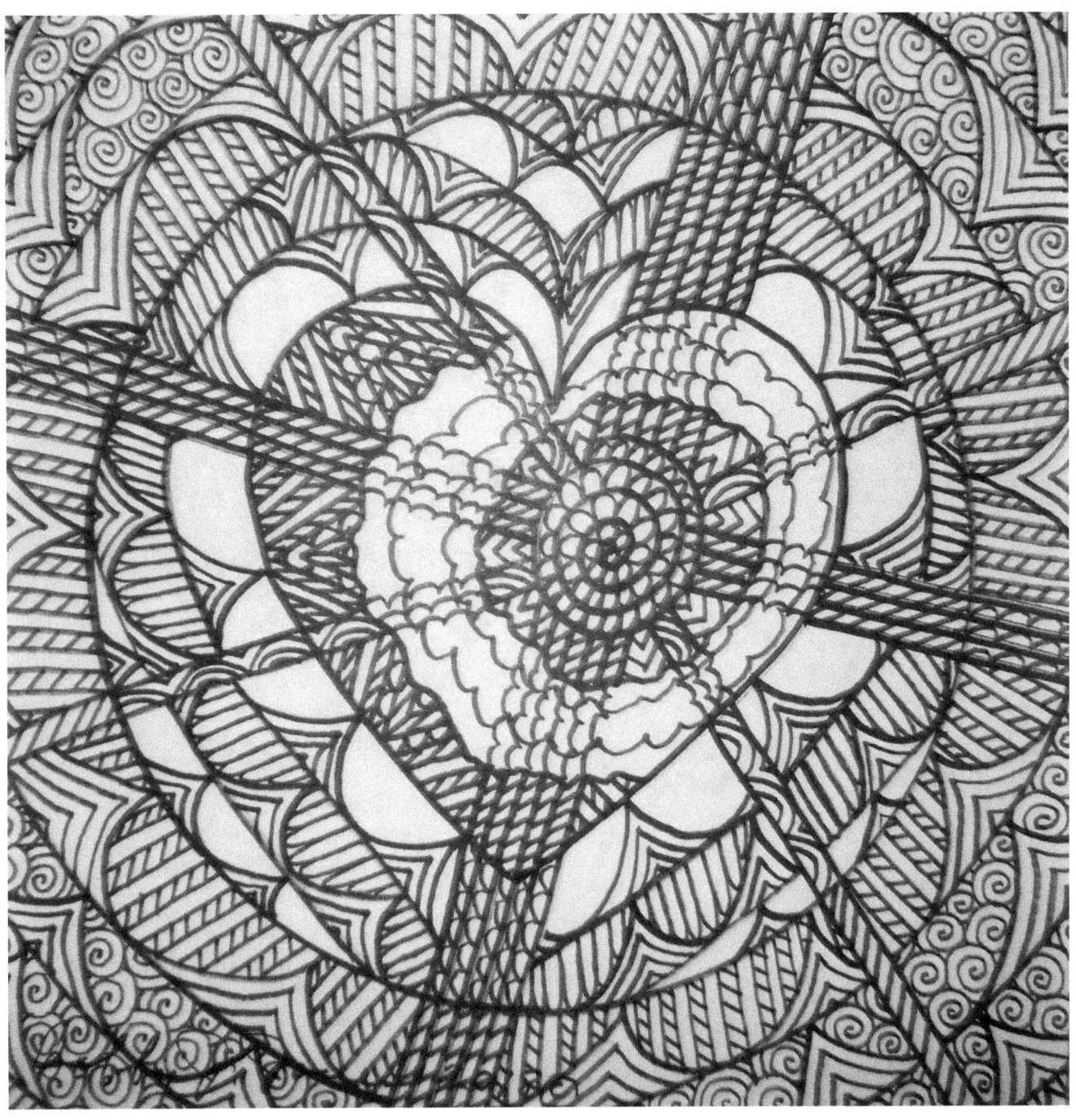

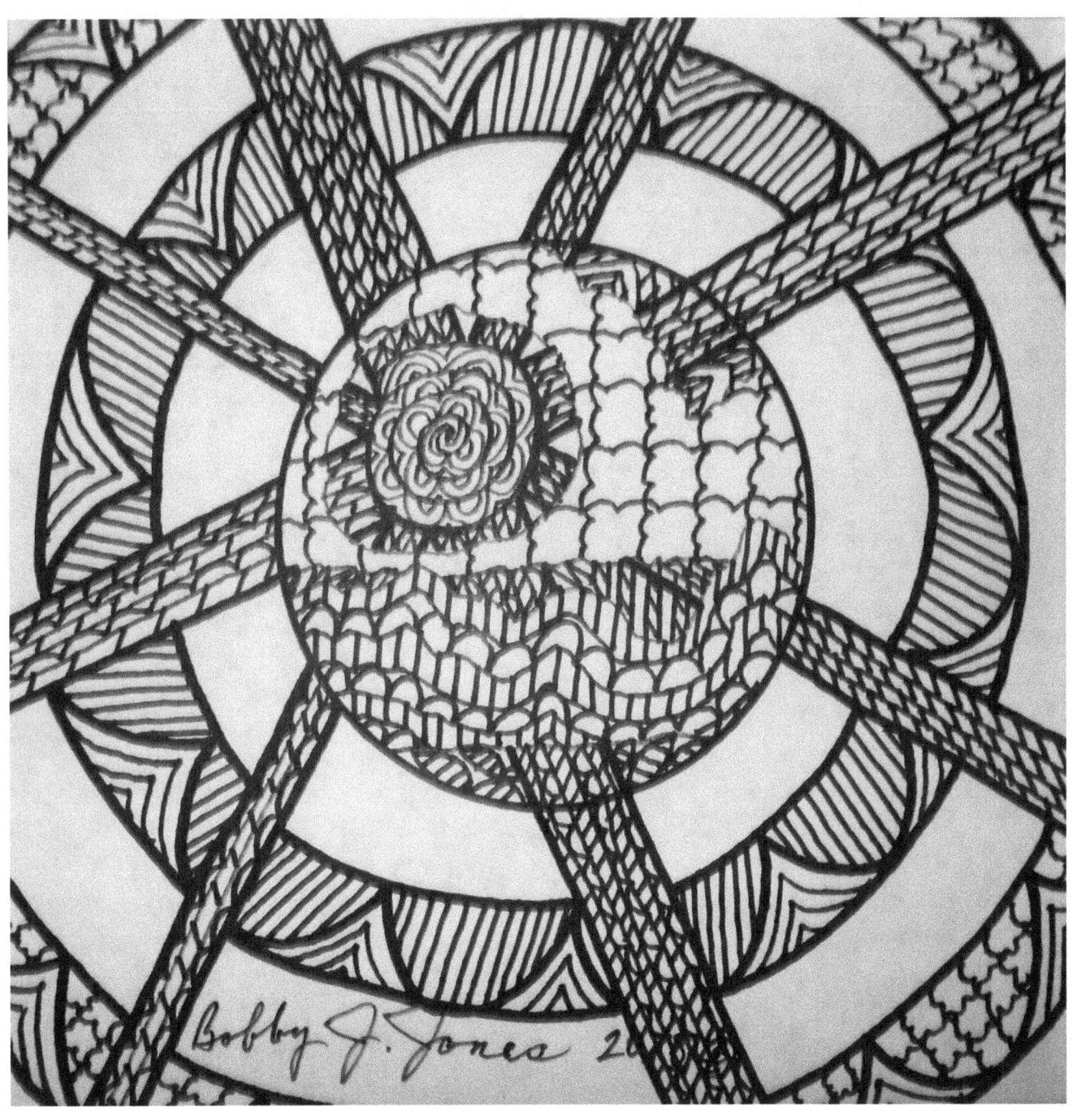

Bobby J. Jones

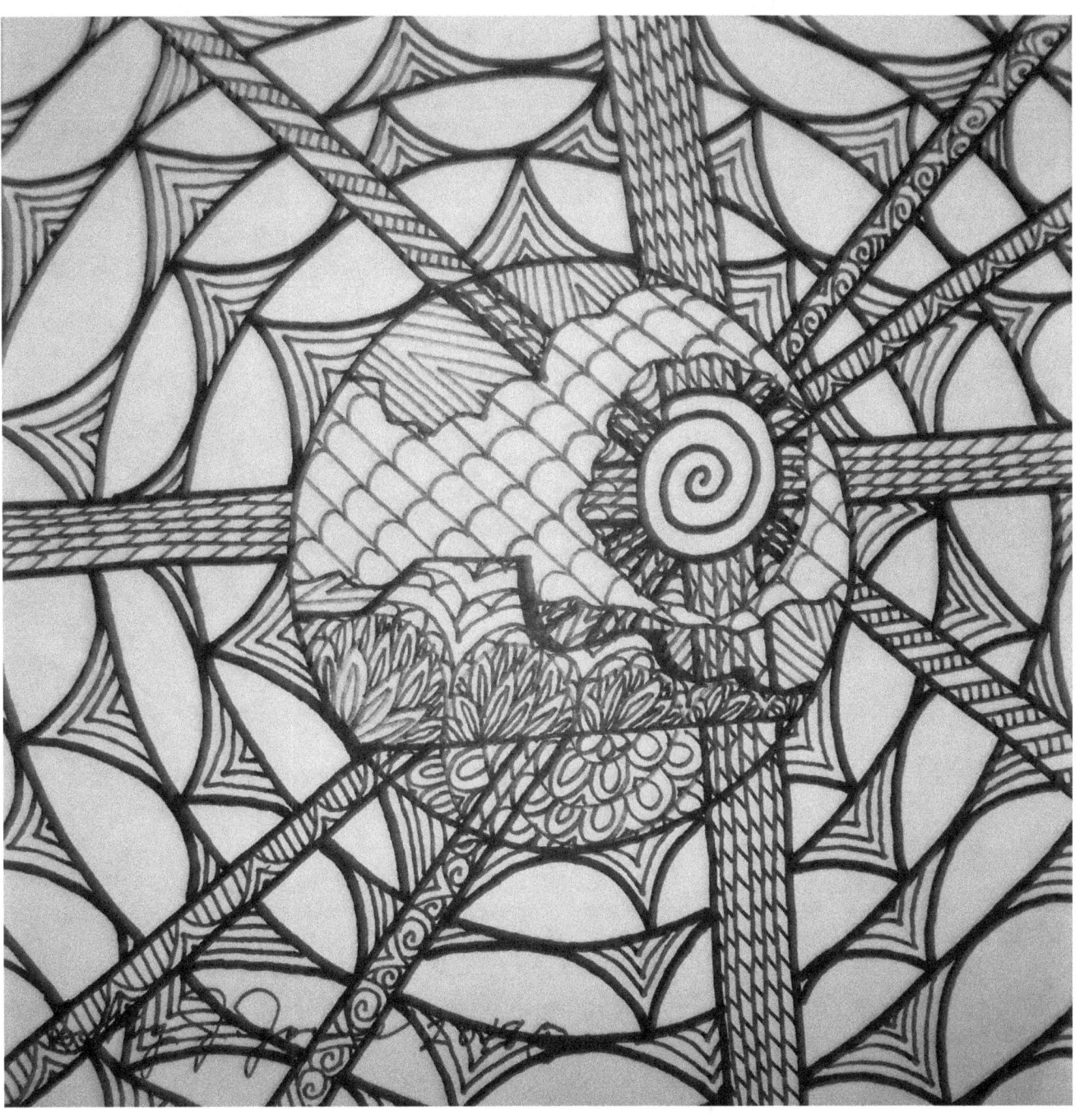

Bobby J. Jones

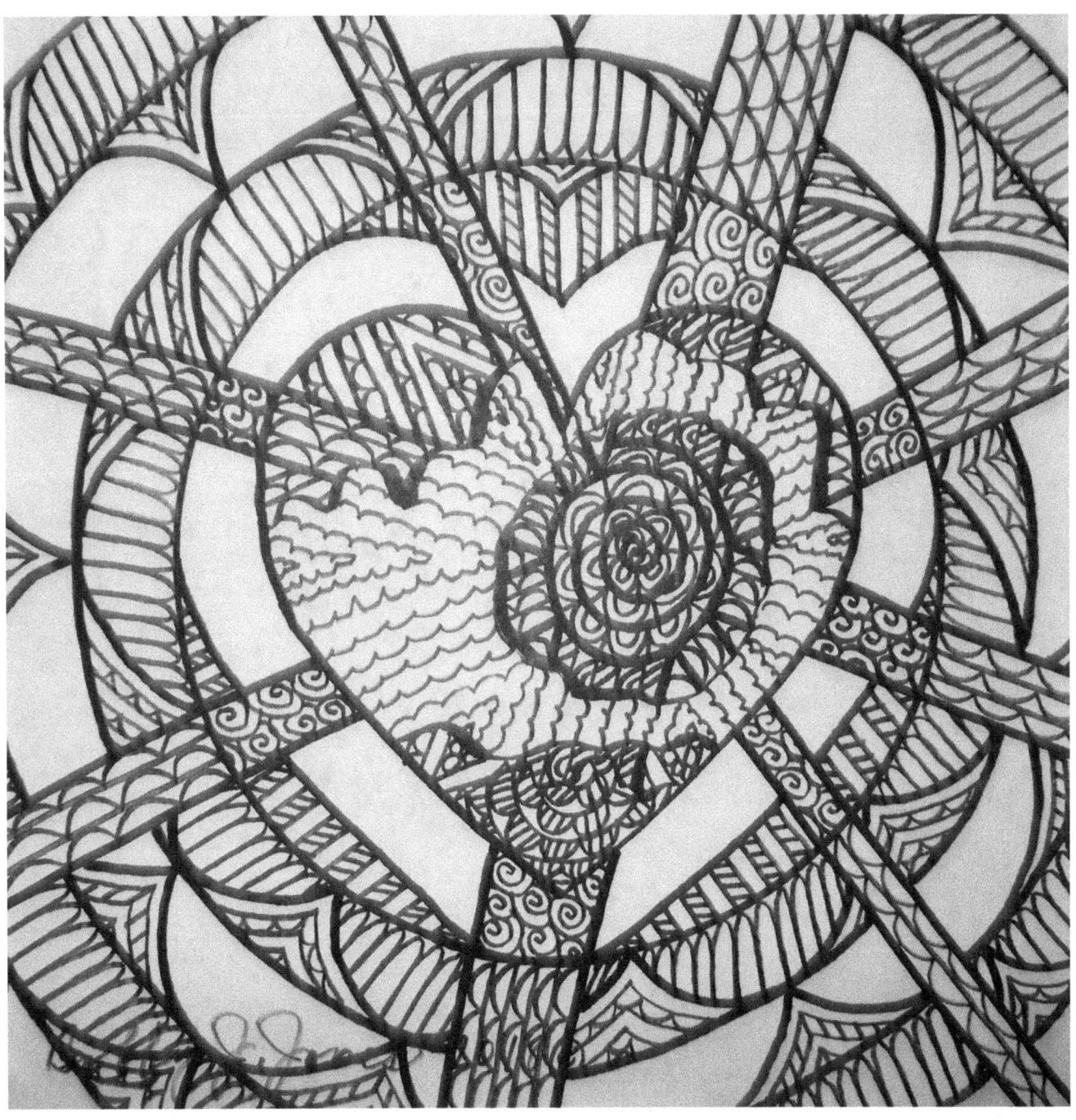

Bobby J. Jones

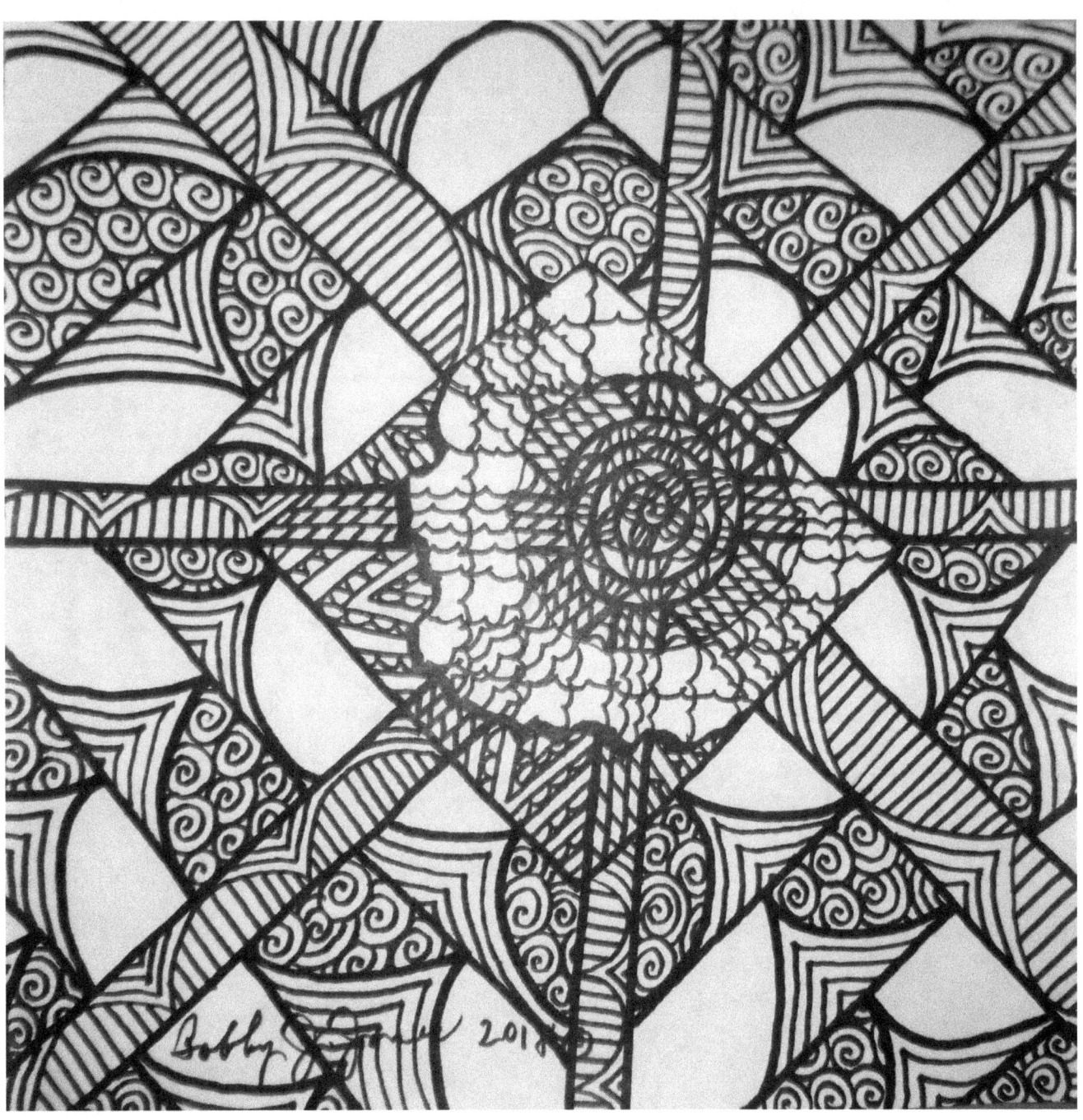

Bobby J. Jones

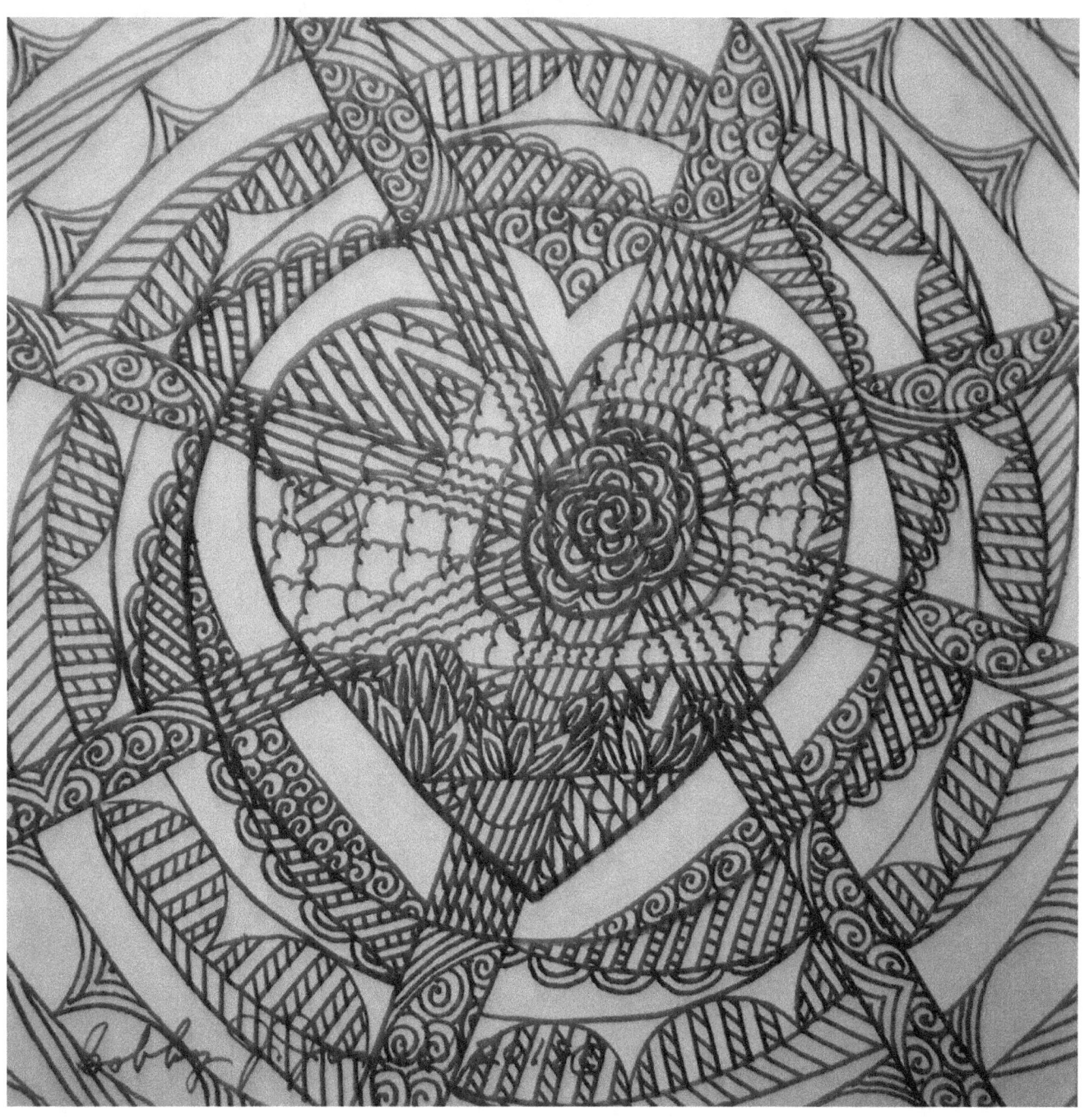

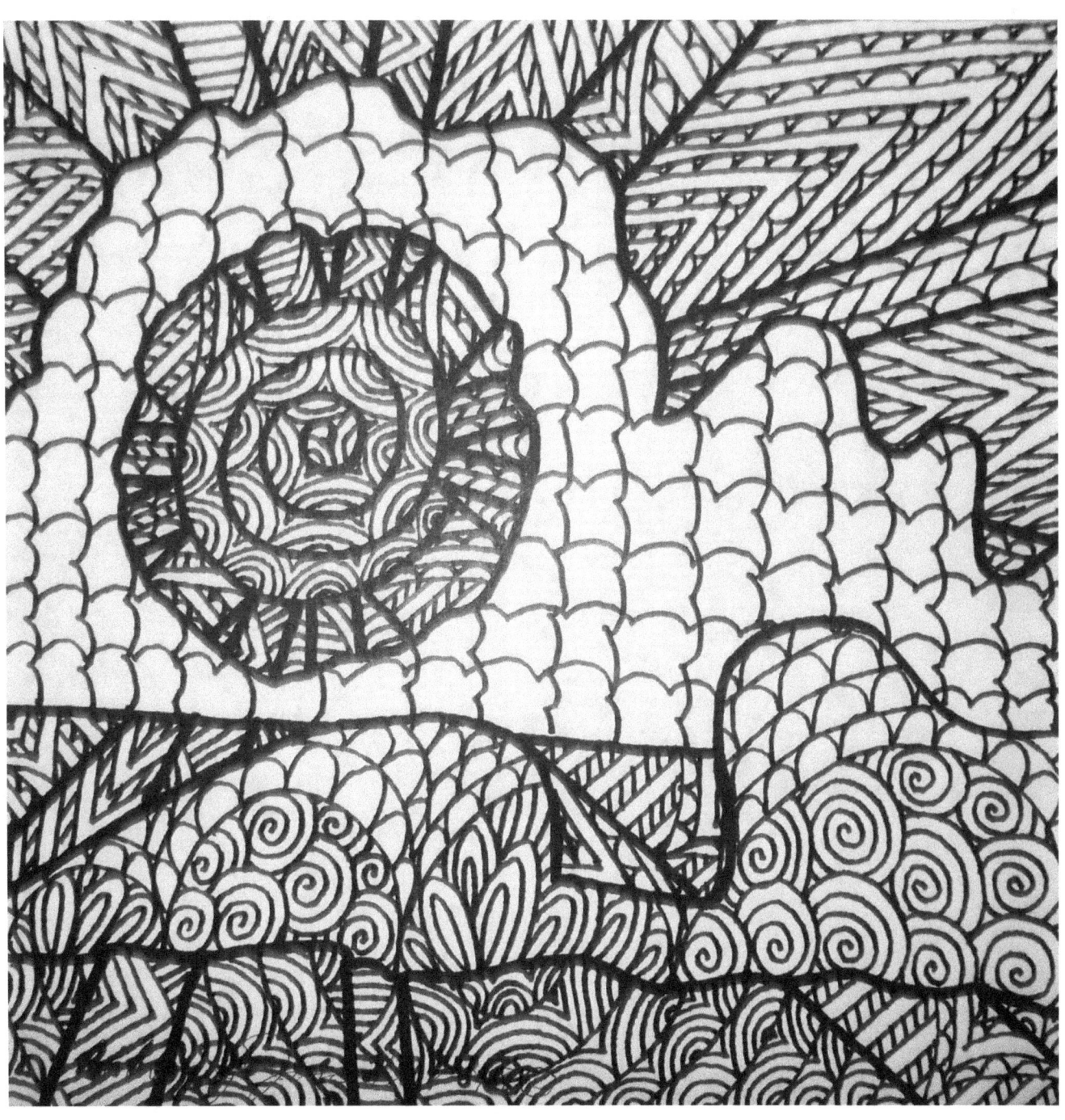

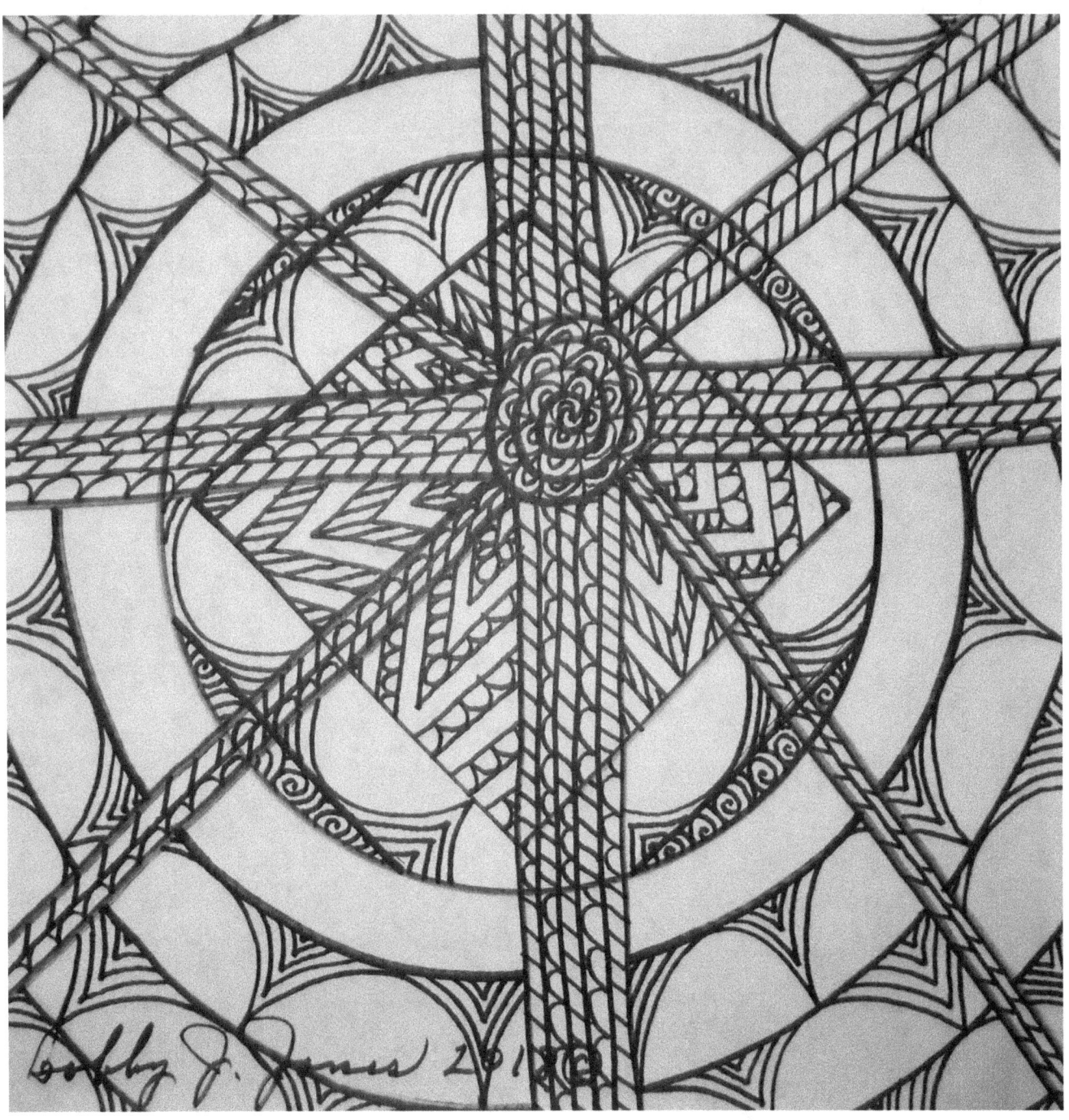

Bobby J. Jones

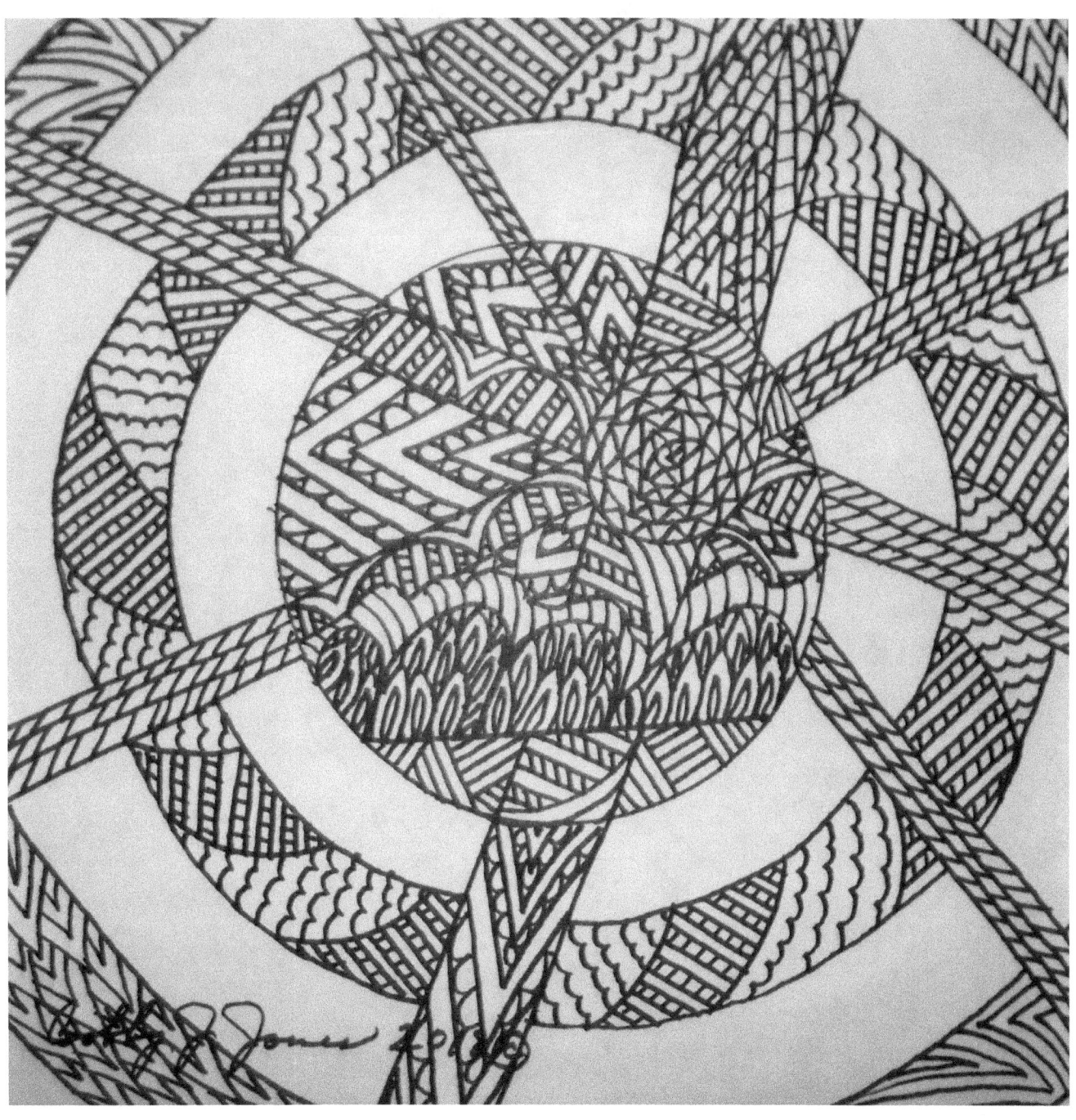

Bobby J. Jones

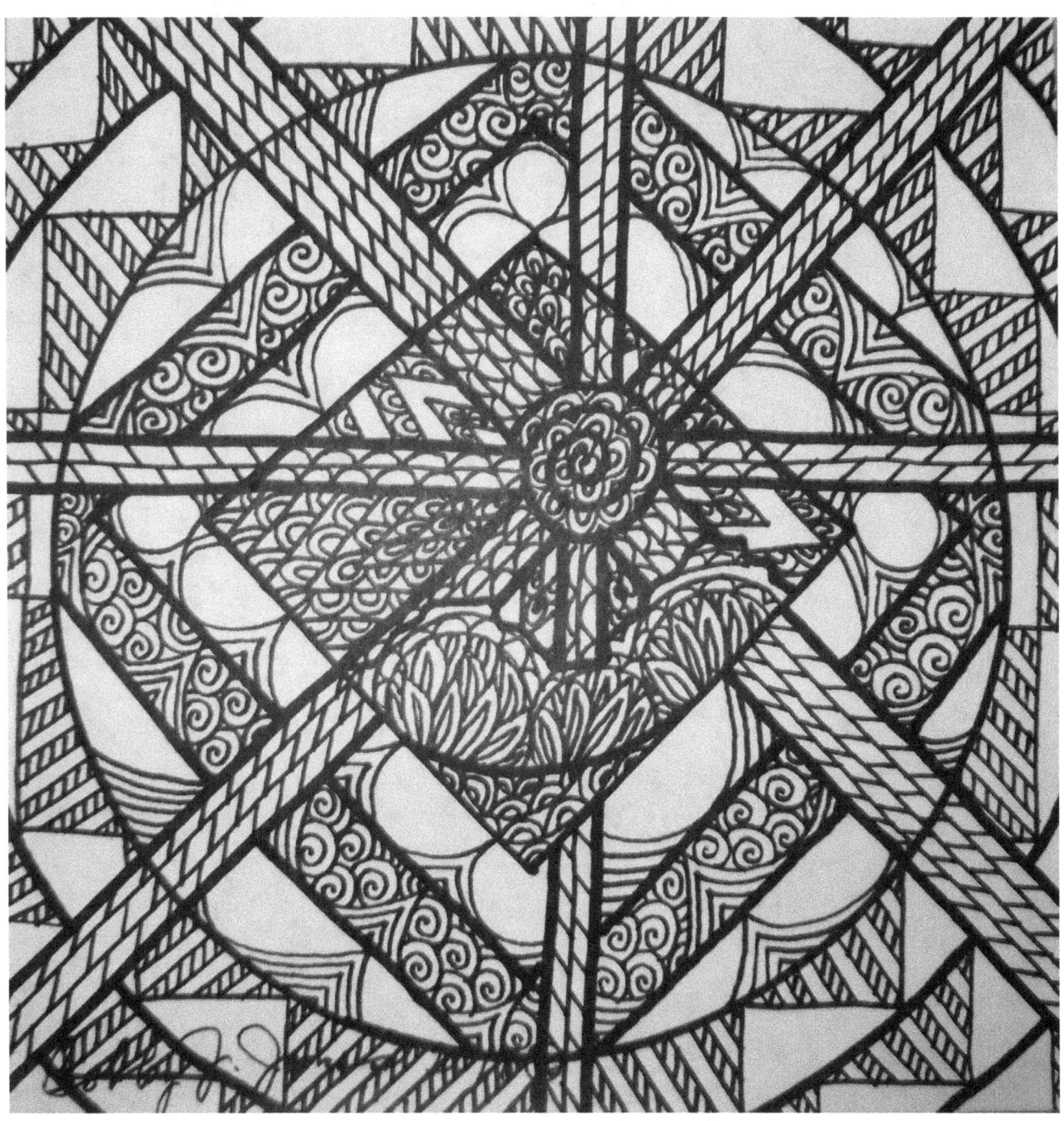

Bobby J. Jones

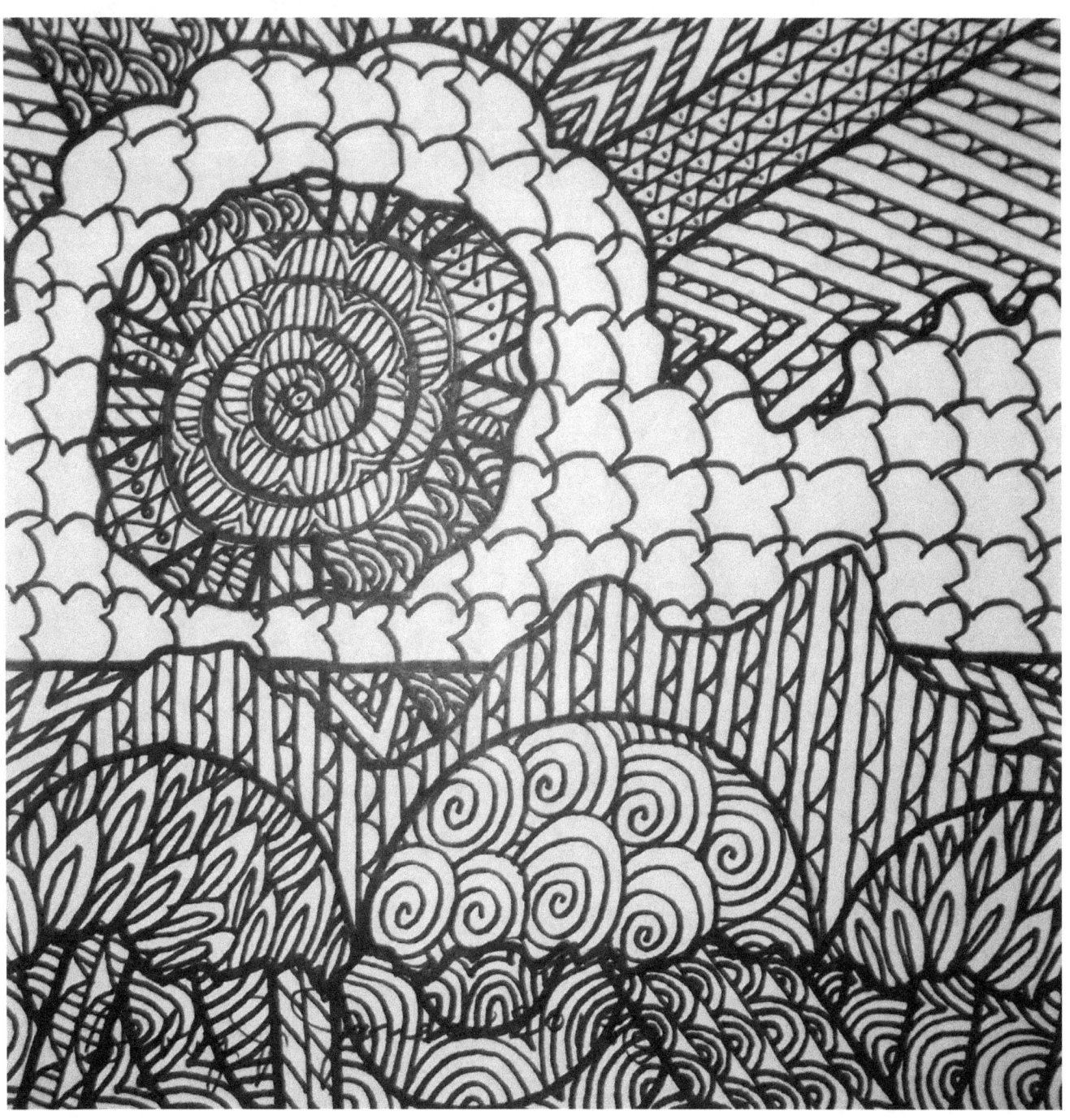

Bobby J. Jones

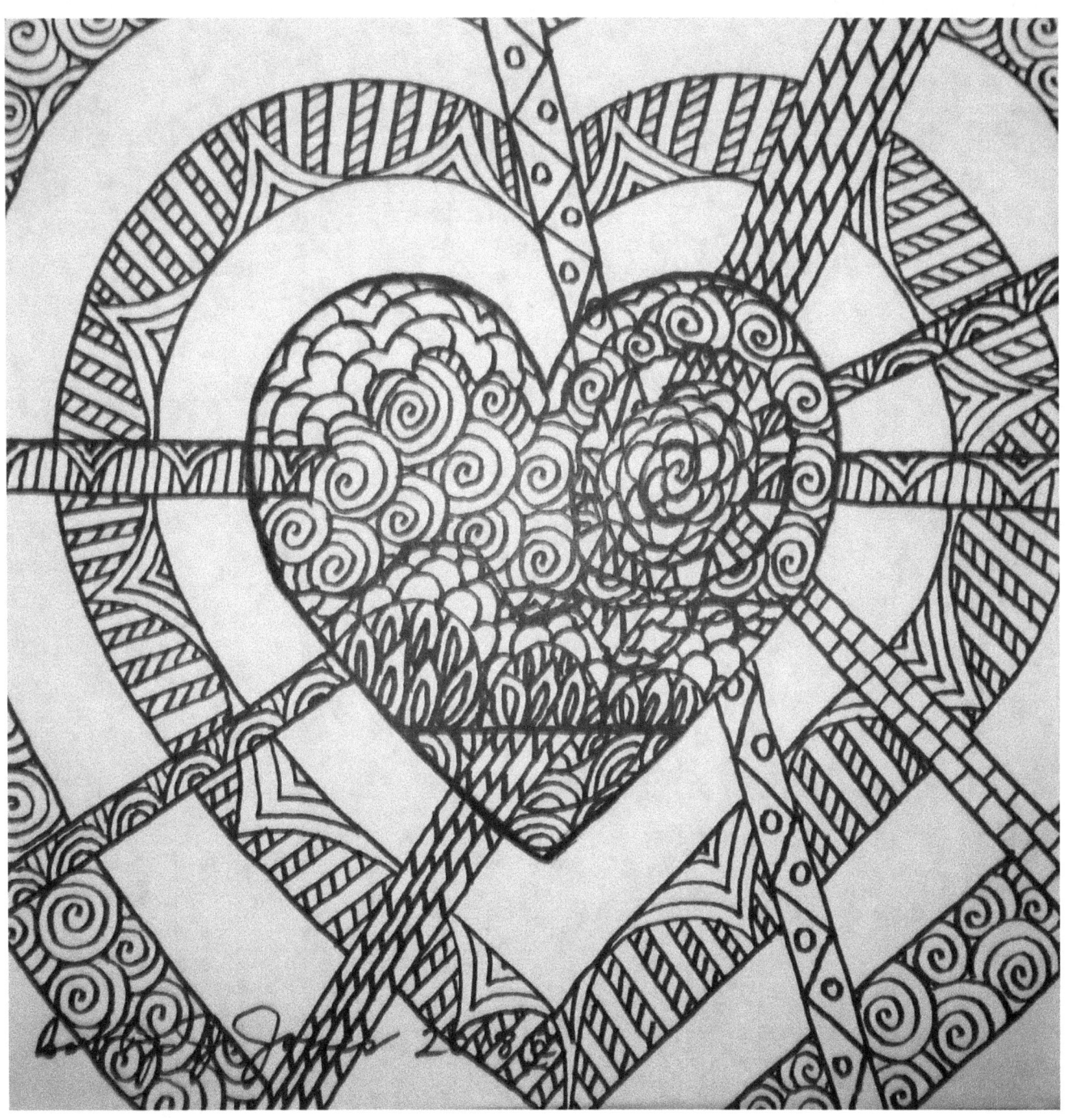

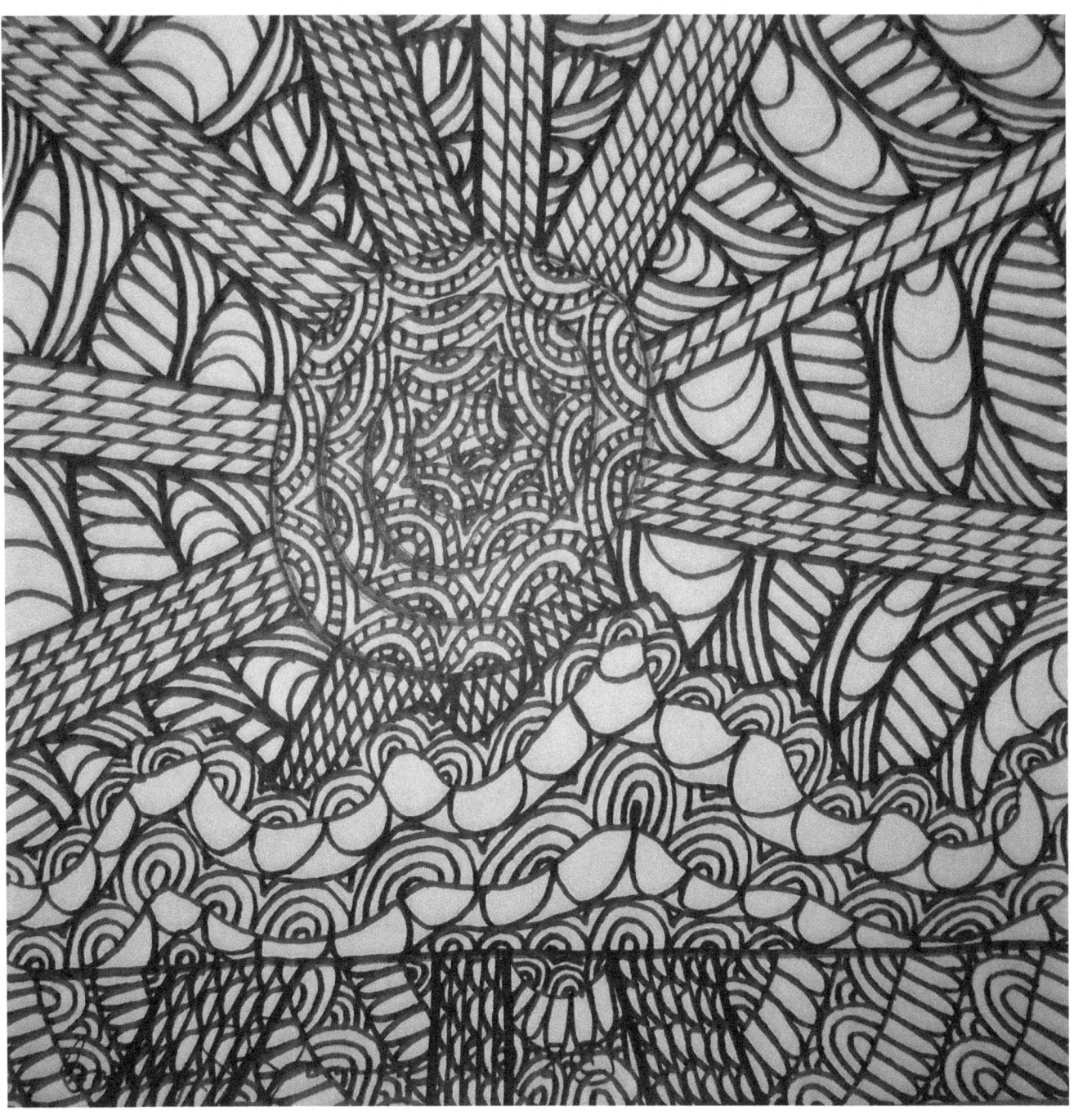

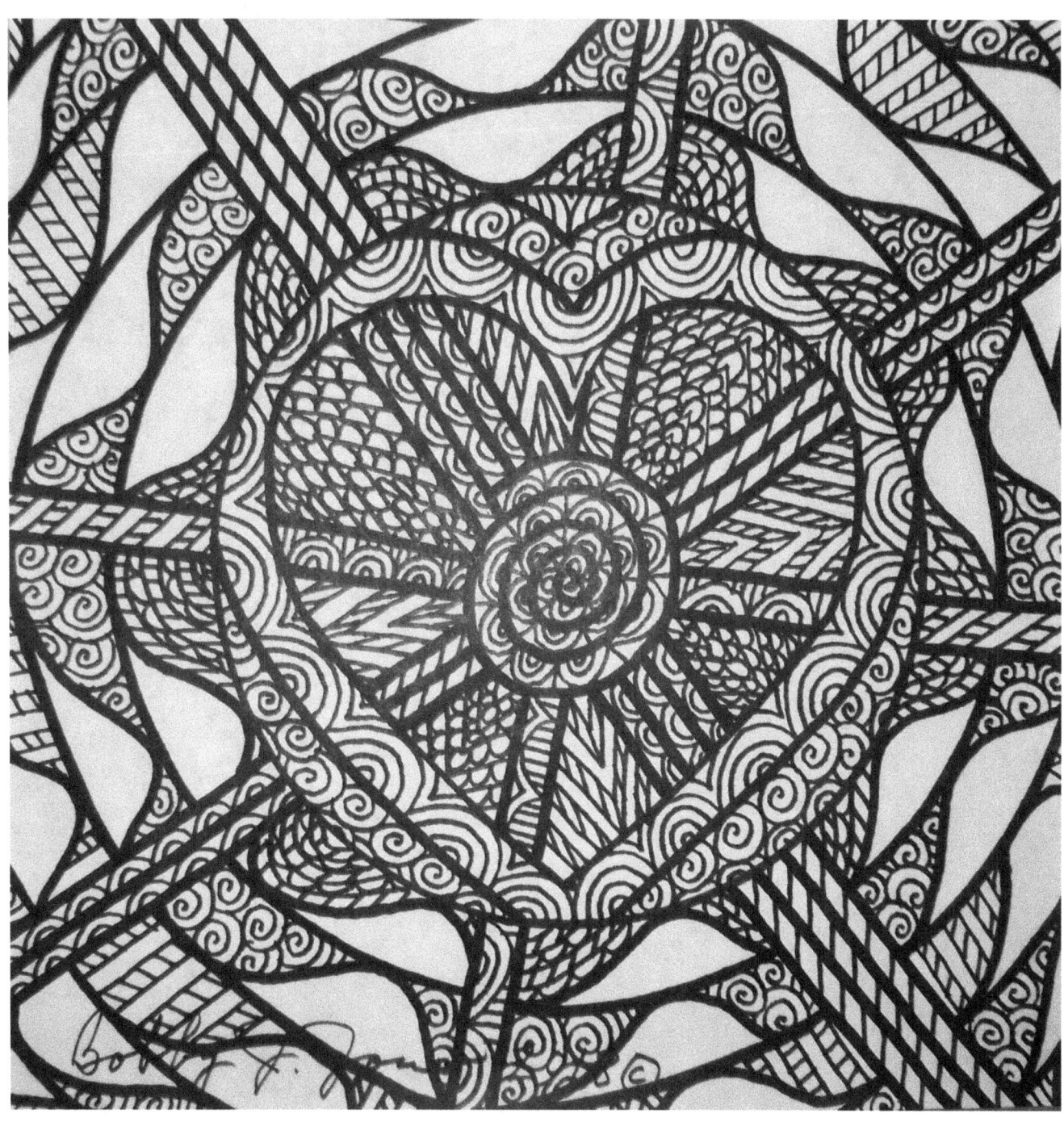

Bobby J. Jones

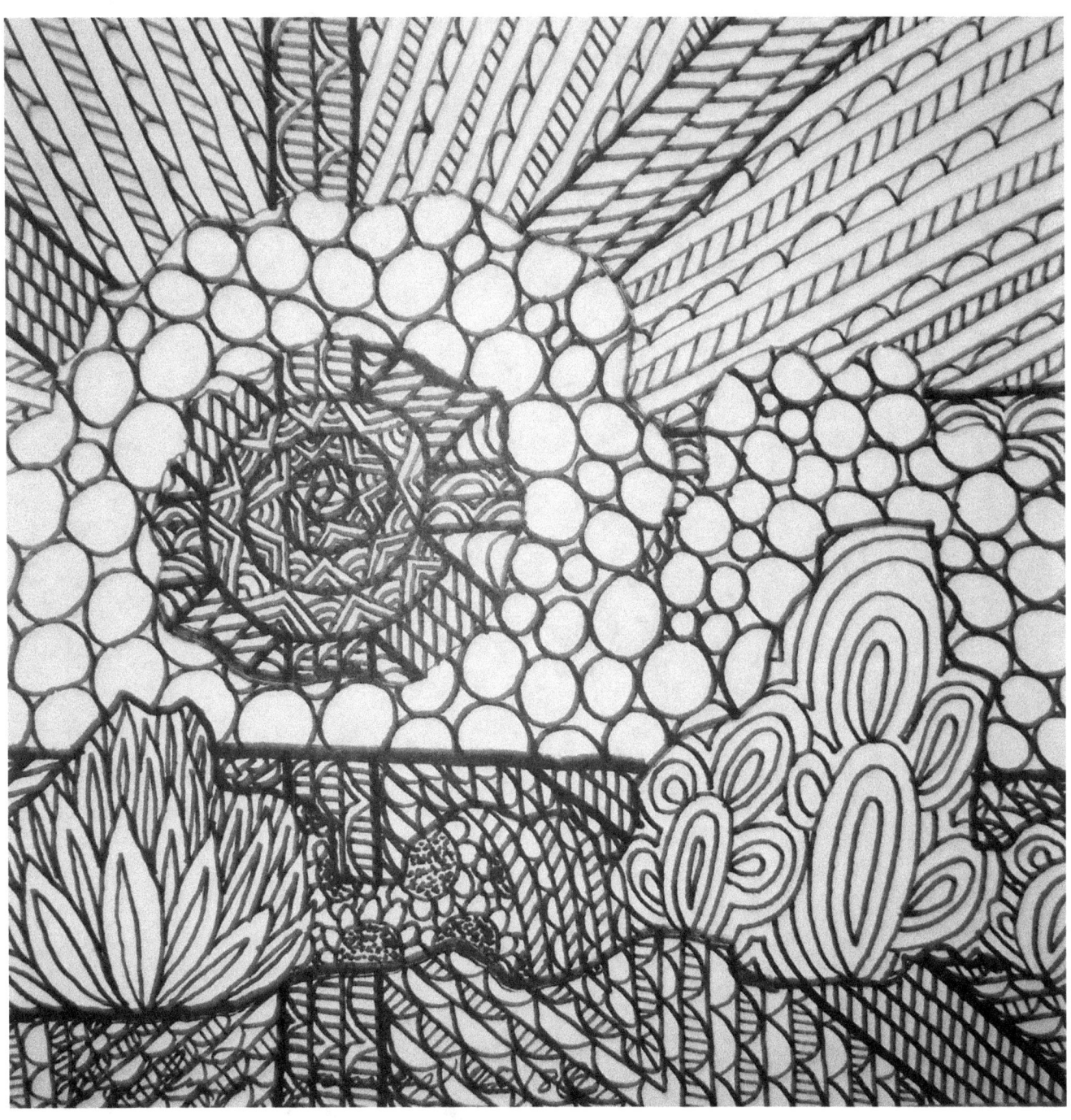

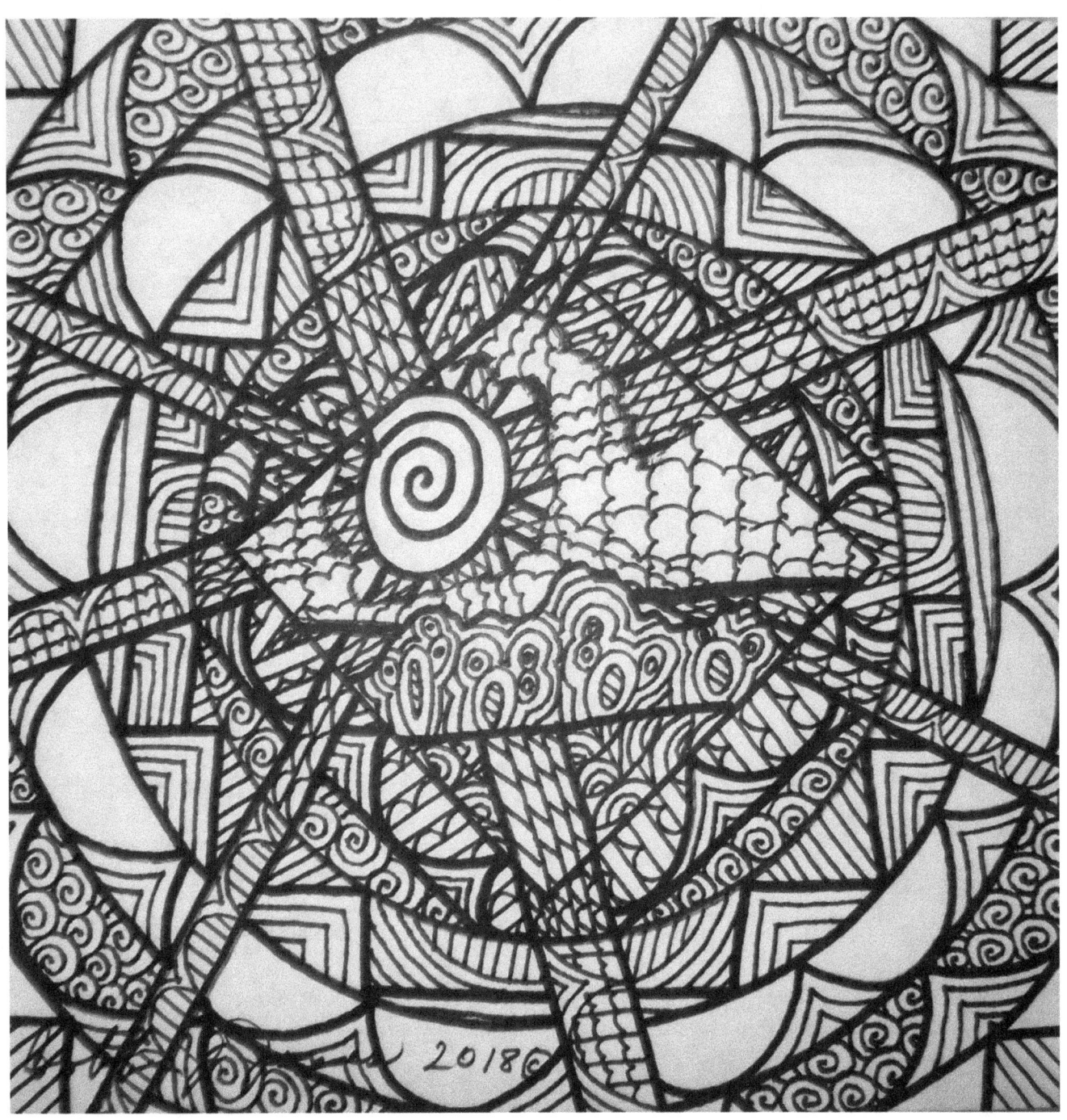

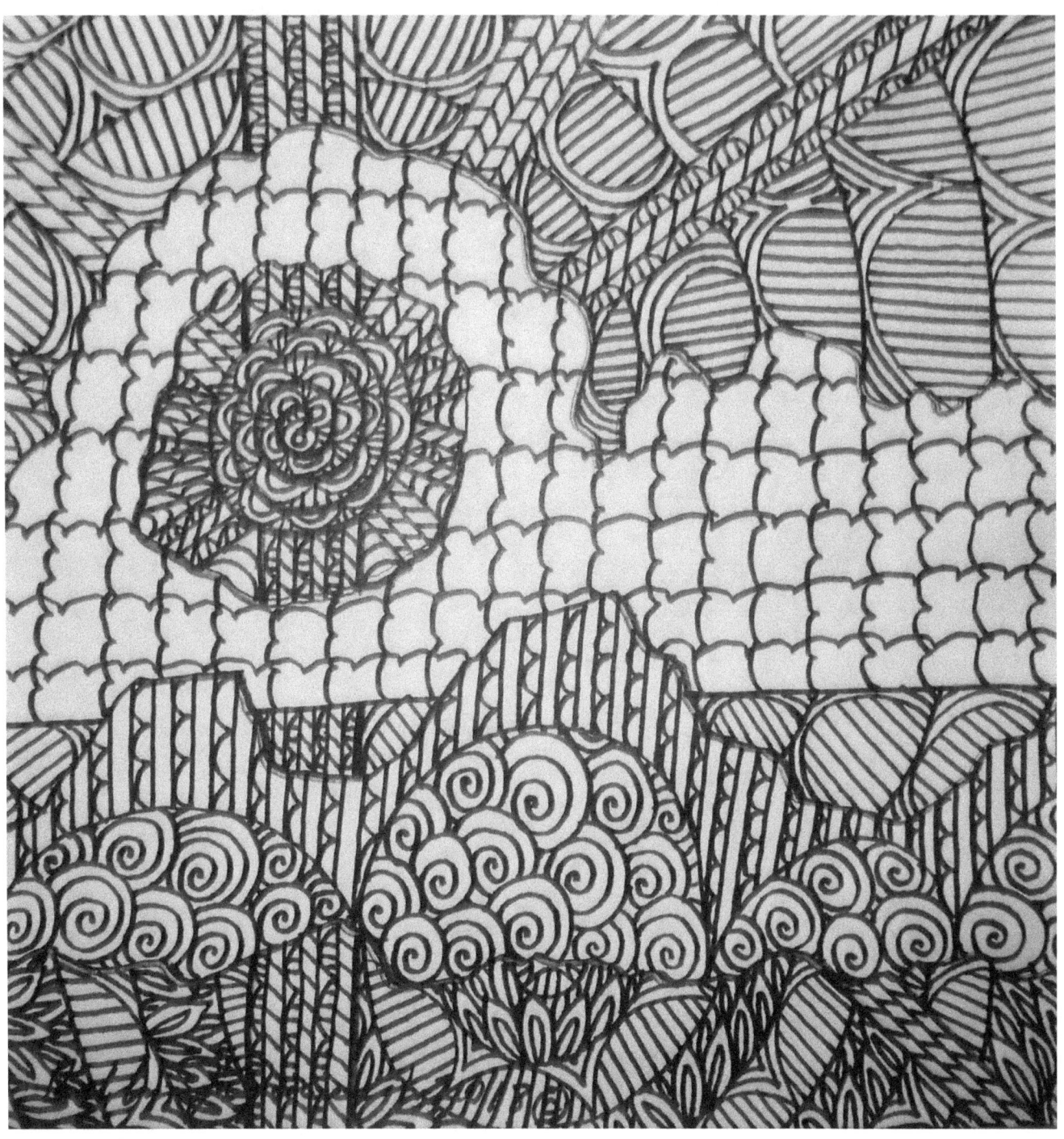

Bobby J. Jones

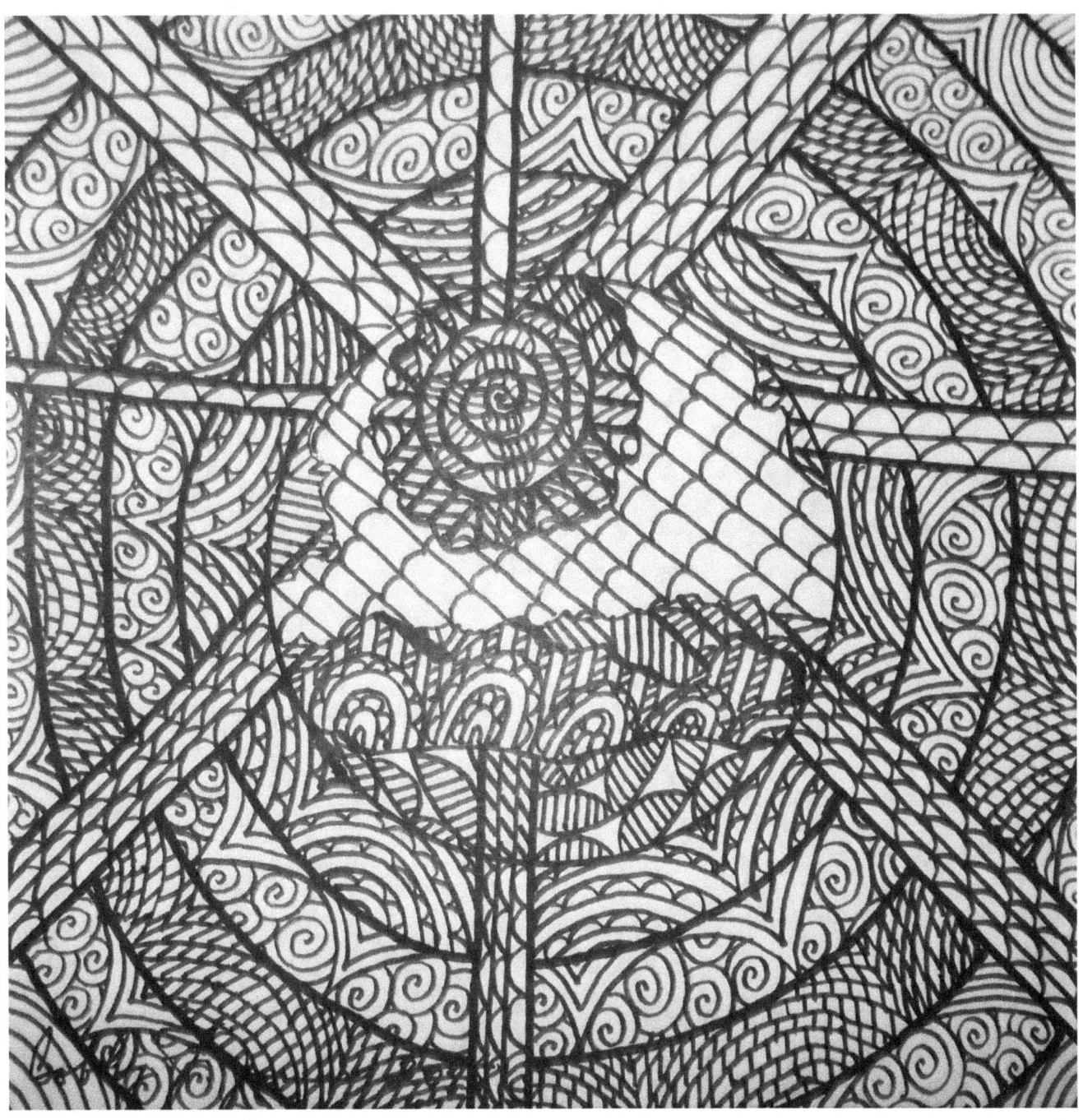

Bobby J. Jones

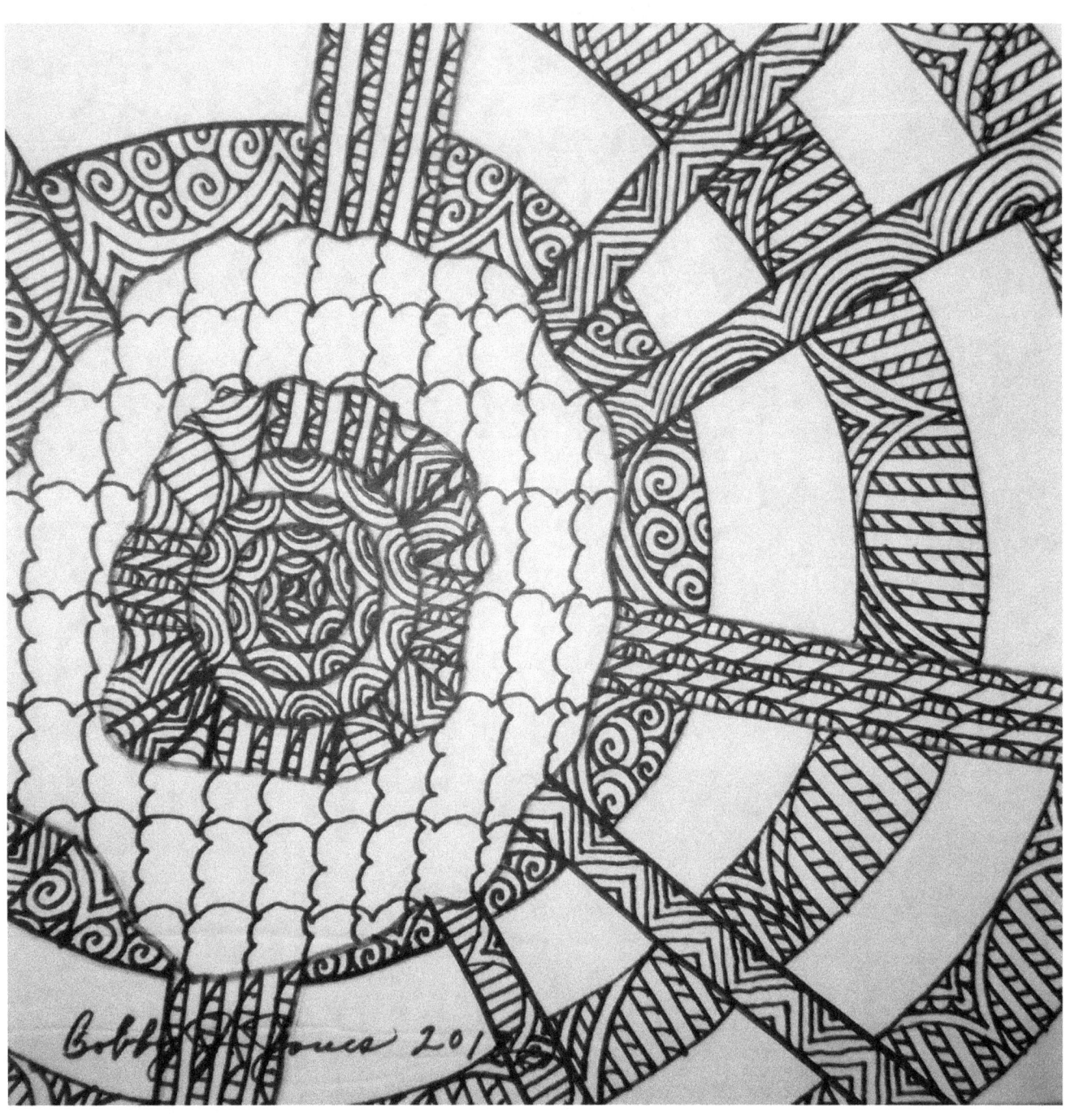

Bobby J. Jones

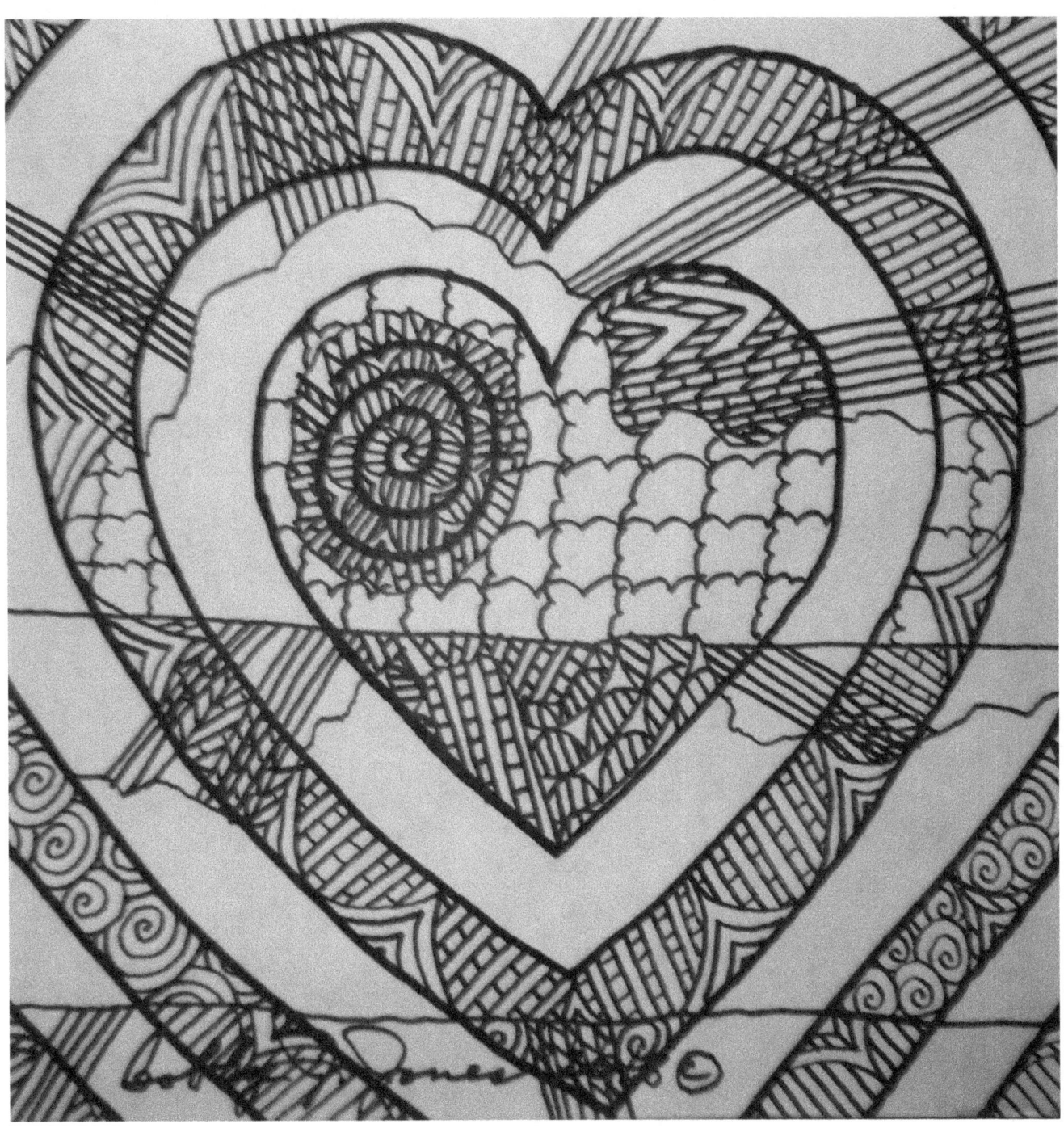

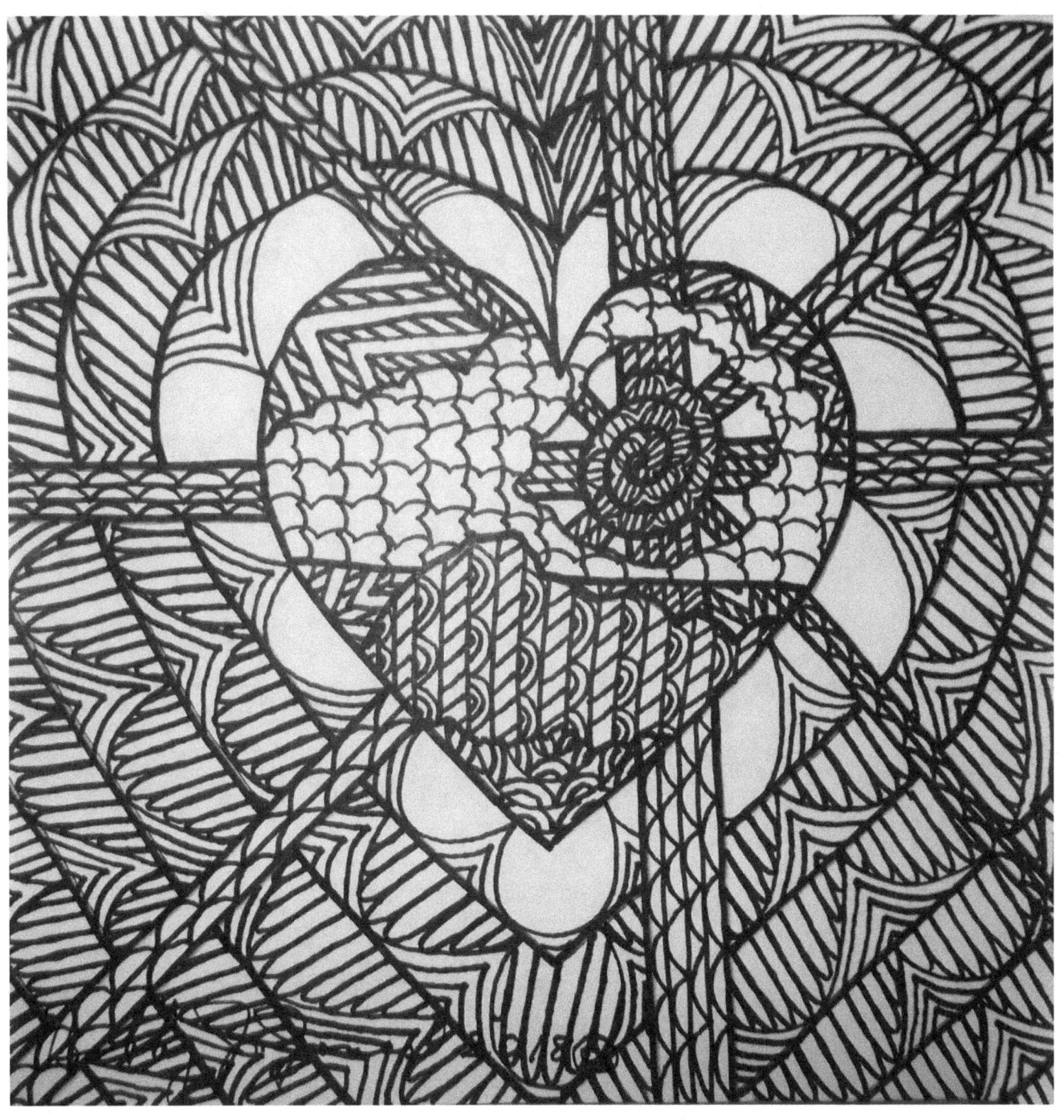

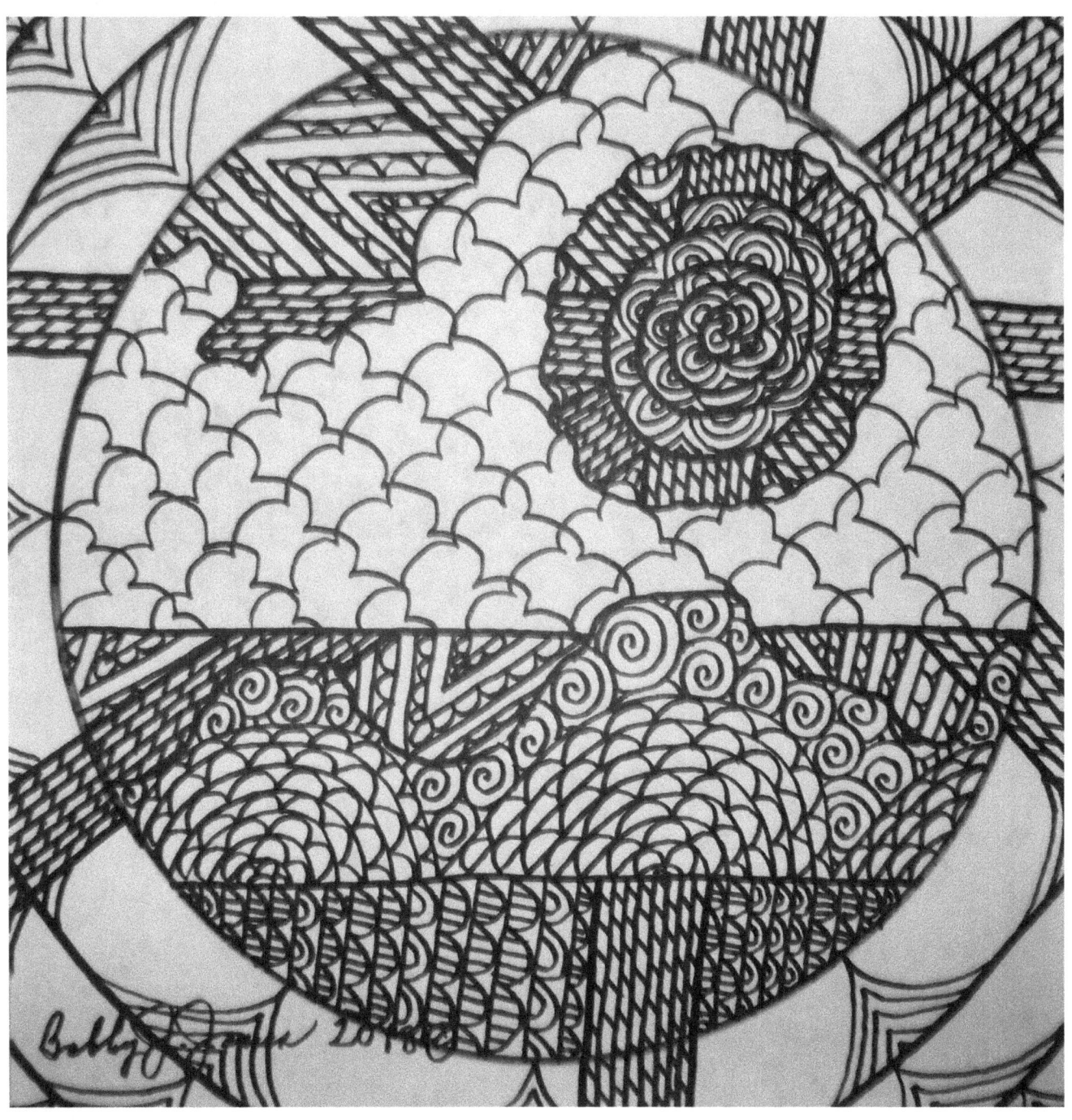

Bobby J. Jones

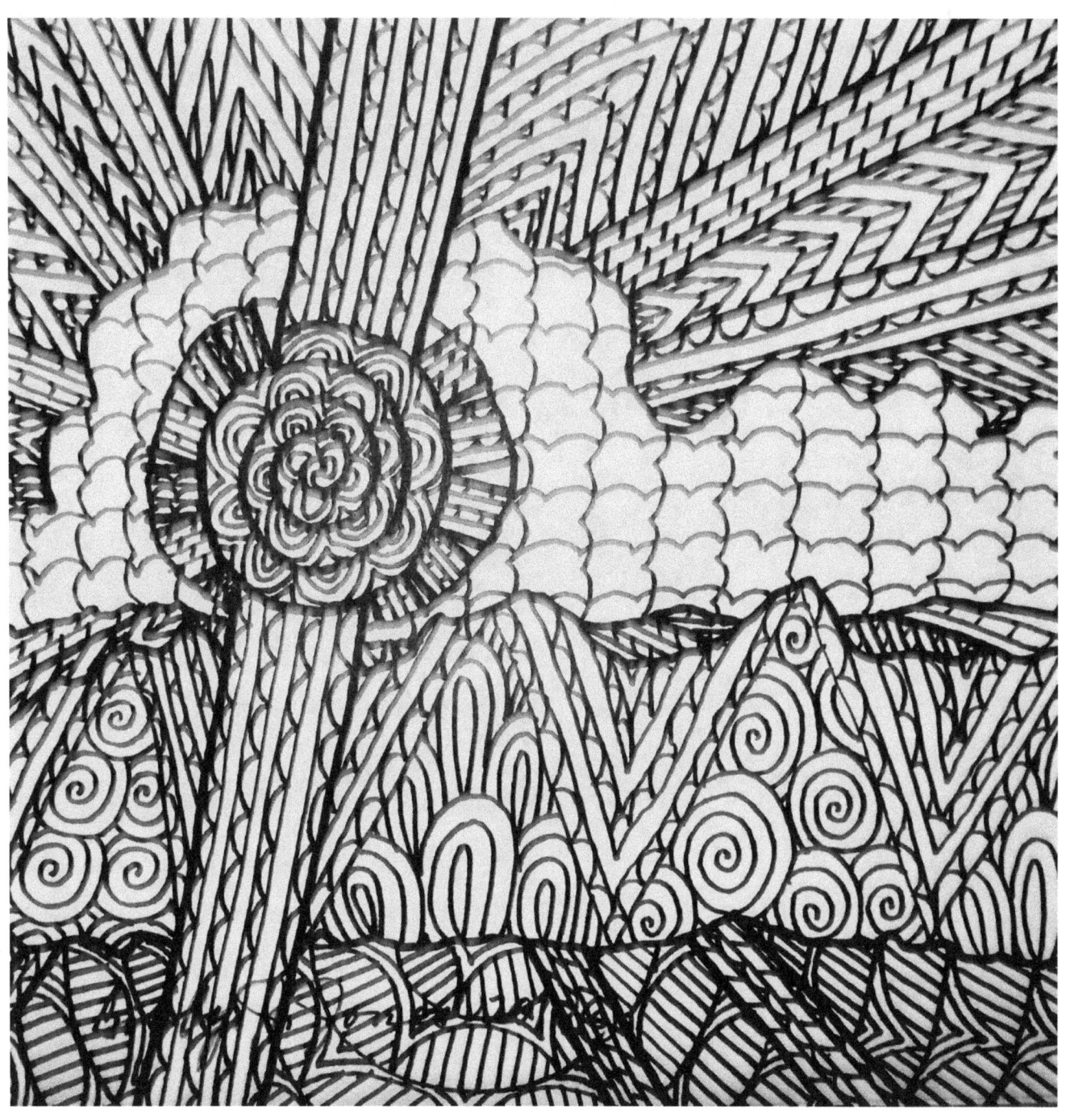

Bobby J. Jones

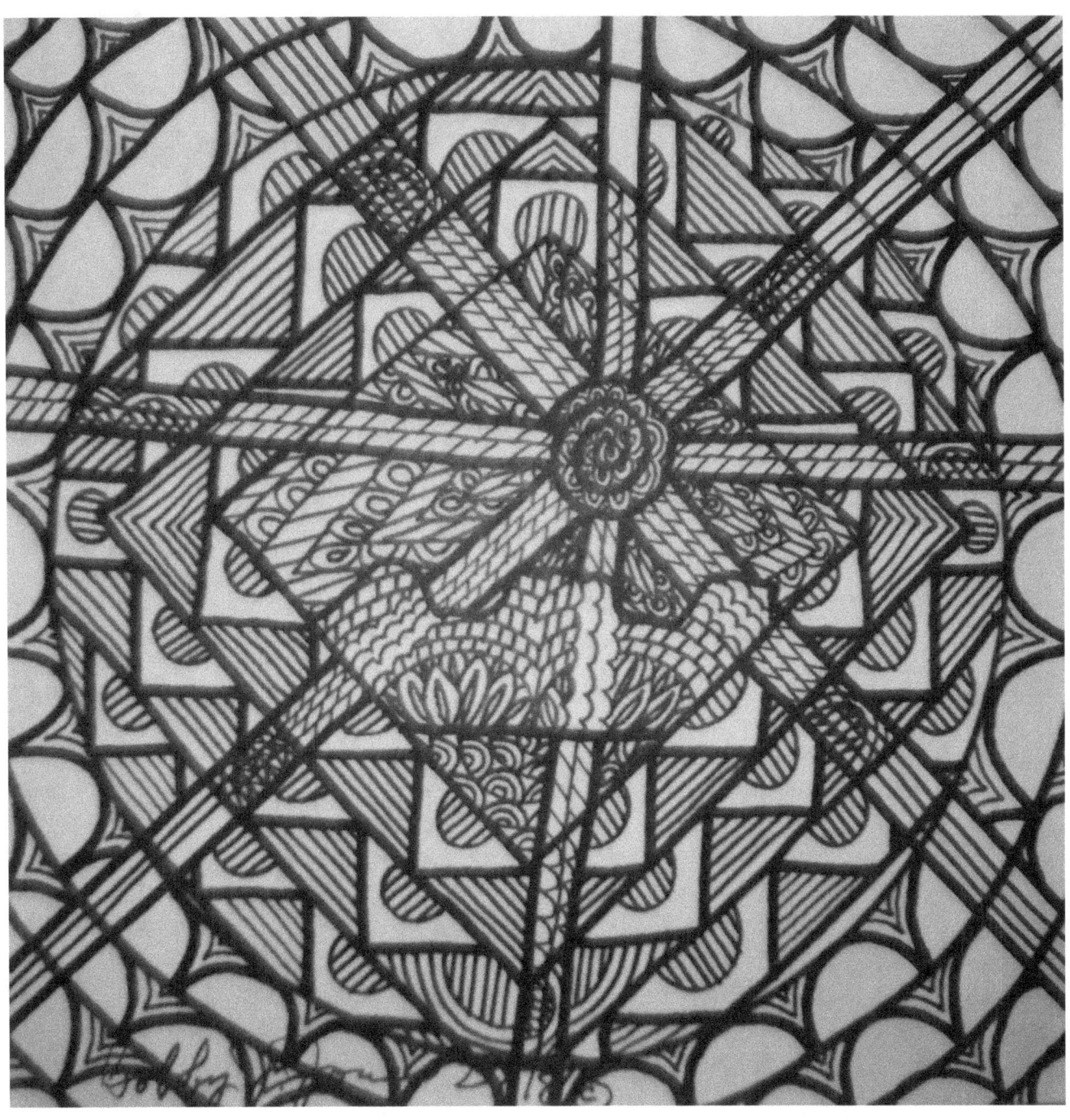

Bobby J. Jones

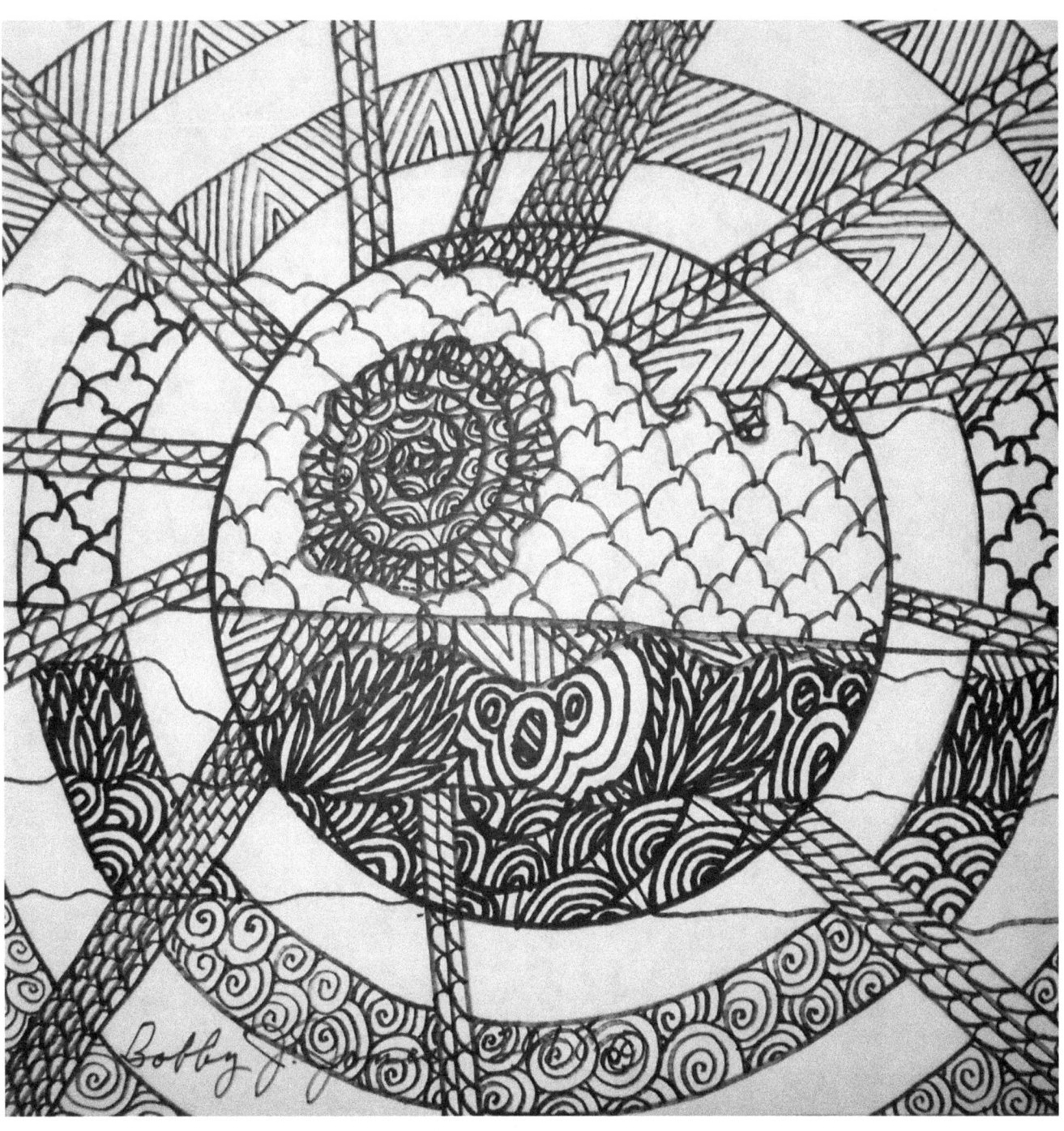

Bobby J. Jones

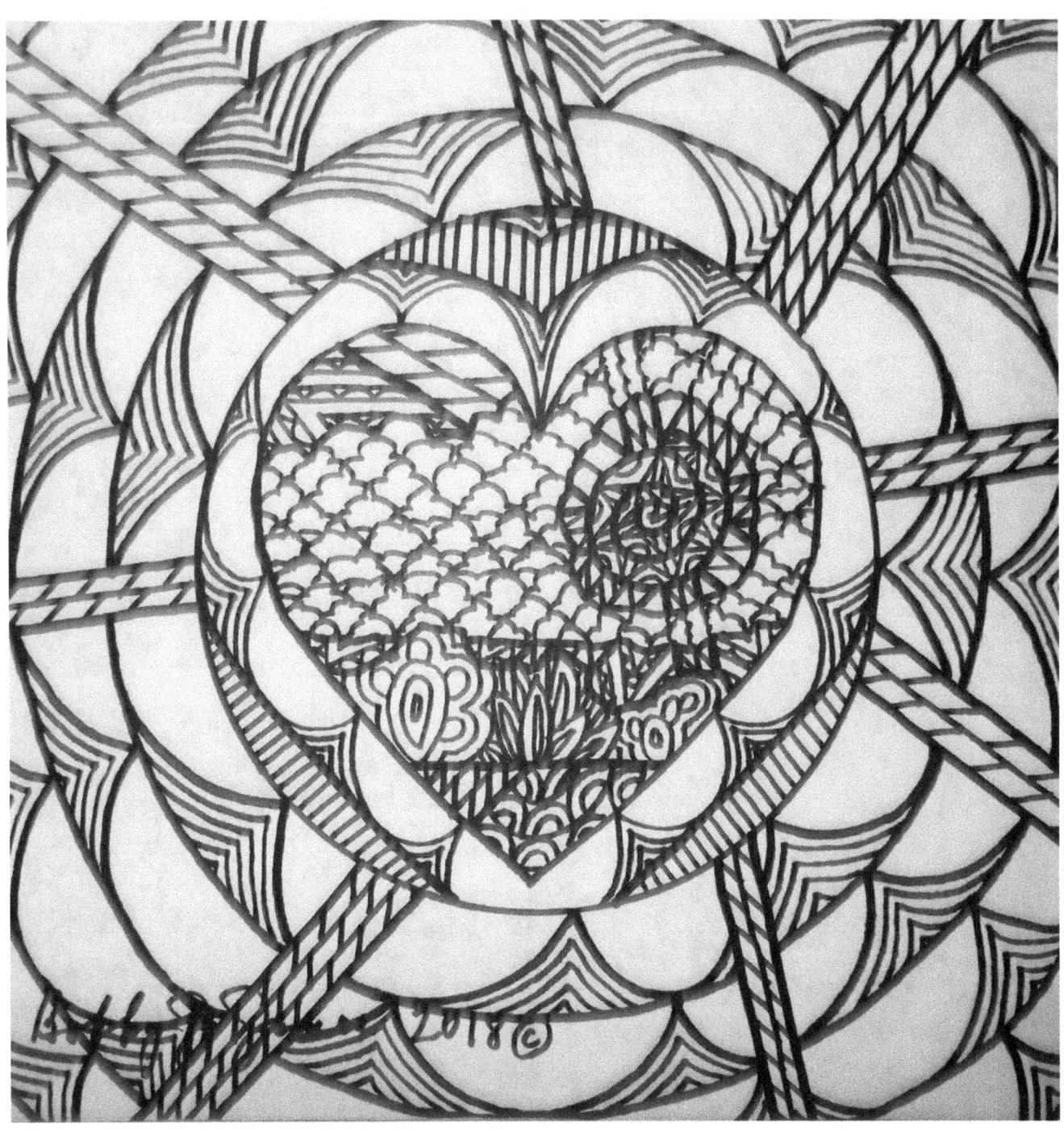

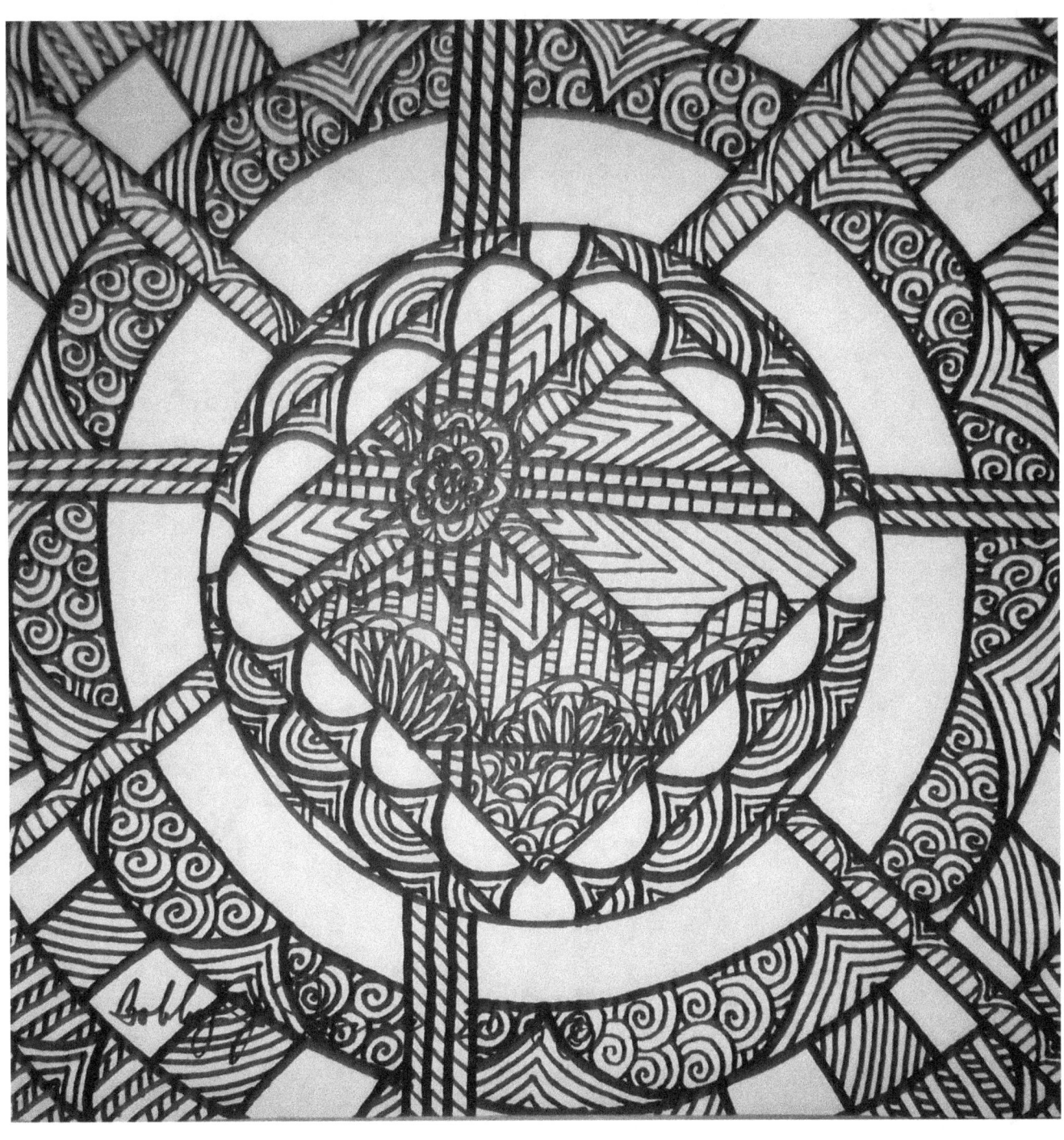

Bobby J. Jones

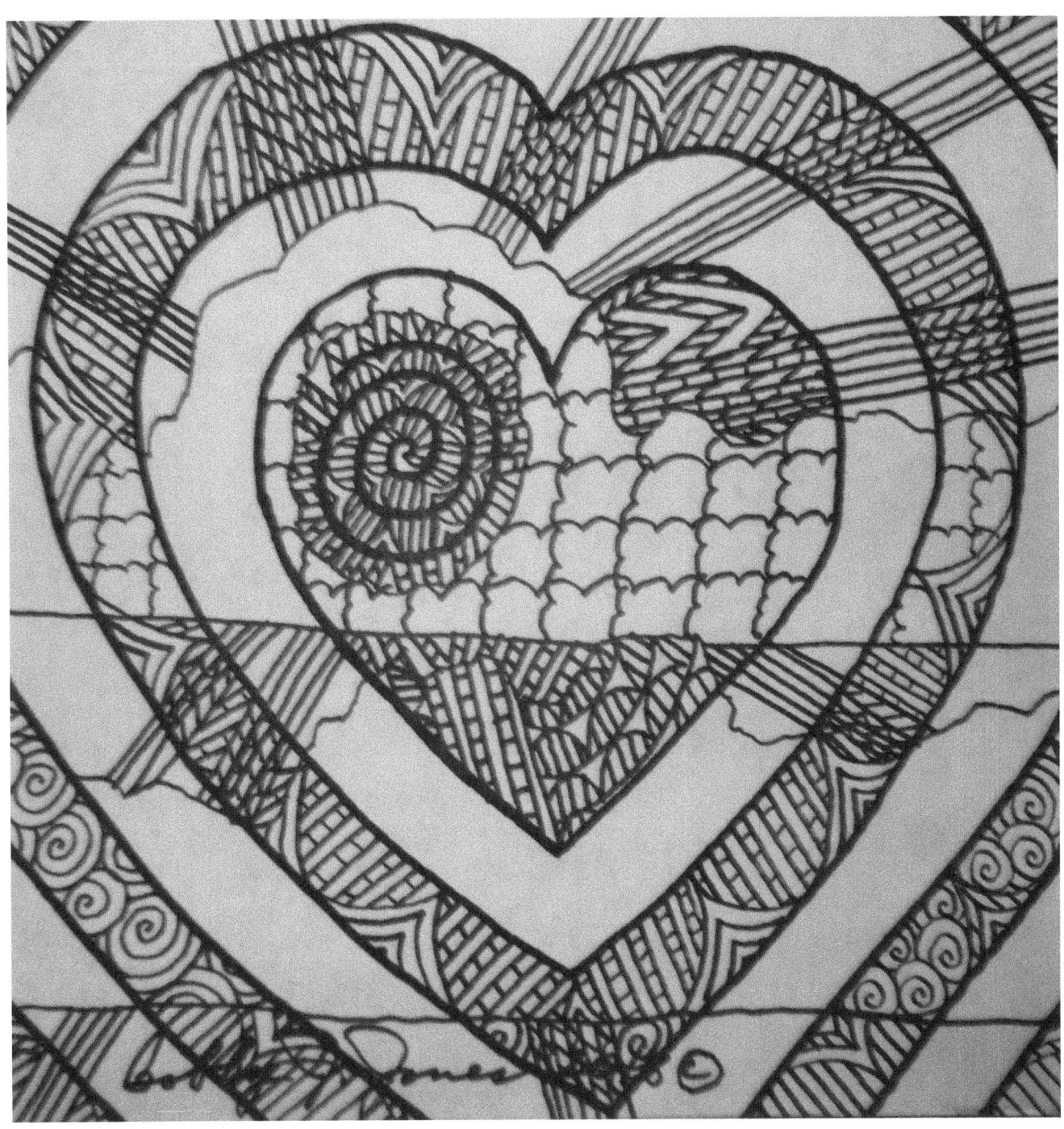

Bobby J. Jones

About The Author:

Bobby Jones was born at Reese Air Force Base in Lubbock, Texas in 1966. His family moved to Fort Worth, Texas in 1968. While growing up in Fort Worth, Texas, Jones attended school in The Fort Worth Independent School District. He graduated from Southwest High School in 1985 with honors.

Jones' father Toney Jones worked for General Dynamics as an Industrial Engineer for 25 years while Bobby's mother Kate Jones taught preschool for 20 years at Wedgwood Methodist Church, which became Genesis United Methodist Church in Fort Worth. Jones is the youngest son out of two daughters and two sons. He has two nieces, two nephews, and two great- grandnephews.

Jones attended Texas Tech University in Lubbock, Texas from 1985-1989. He received a BFA in Studio Art (Painting and Drawing) with honors in 1989. Bobby was a member of Alpha Phi Omega at Texas Tech and Golden Key. Then he attended The University of New Mexico in Albuquerque, NM. He obtained a Masters of Art in Art Education (Museum Education, Ceramics, and Photography) in 1994.

Bobby moved to Southern California in 1997 and worked in retail management from 1999 to 2009 for various retail companies in the Palm Springs area. Jones returned to New Mexico in 2009. He worked in the customer service profession from 2010 to 2014.

Jones attended Central New Mexico Community College. Bobby obtained an Alternative Teaching Degree in Special Education and was inducted into Phi Theta Kappa. He started working for Albuquerque Public Schools as a substitute teacher in Special Education.

He is currently an Educational Assistant in Special Education in Albuquerque, New Mexico with The Albuquerque Public Schools. Jones plans to become a teacher in New Mexico. He is also a member of First Unitarian Church in Albuquerque.

Jones is also an artist and creates two dimensional mixed media art that consists of his painting and drawing skills. His artistic inspiration focuses upon the environment of New Mexico. He has exhibited his work at The Factory on 5th, The Tortuga Gallery, The 606 Gallery, and First Unitarian Church's Social Hall.

He is currently preparing for an art exhibit at The South Broadway Cultural Center in January and June, 2019. His art entry for The 28th ArtsThrive Exhibit was accepted by the art jury members. Three art pieces will be on display at The Albuquerque Museum starting October 19, 2018 in New Mexico.

His artwork appeared in The Desert Sun newspaper (Palm Springs, CA) in the special edition of the first year anniversary of 9/11 and the 40th anniversary of The Kennedy Assassination. Jones also created an art gallery on Facebook, Bobbo66Art Gallery. He invites everyone to look at his art creations.

The artist freehands these original images in this coloring book. Jones does not use computer software programs, rulers or t-squares to create these beautiful images. He enjoys seeing the imperfections in his work. The imperfections are what make Jones' work uniquely original. Jones suggests to the people that buy this book. They can doodle on the blank pages opposite the blackline images or create their own dreamscapes. He is creating a series of coloring books and is creating images for a second coloring book for children of all ages.